She Is Just Getting Started

To my big sis!
Hope you love my story.
Stay Butterfly Strong!
♡ Patti

She Is Just Getting Started

For permission requests, write to
GCW Publishing House at:
team@thegreatcanadianwoman.ca
Published by GCW Publishing House and Media Group
www.gcwpublishing.com

Quantity sales. Special discounts are available on quantity purchases by corporations, associations, and others.
For details, contact the GCW Publishing House and Media Group head office at the address above.

Paperback ISBN 978-1-990370-04-5
eBook ISBN 978-1-990370-05-2

Edited by Christine Stock
Book Designed by Doris Chung
Cover Designed by Michelle Fairbanks
eBook by Ellie Silpa

Printed in North America

She Is Just Getting Started

A collection of real-life stories from women who chose to step into their power, navigate the world of uncertainty, rewrite the story of what "success" means to them, and embark on their entrepreneurial path — stories that will help inspire future generations of women in their transition to entrepreneurship.

Aisha Saintiche . Crystal Mank
Danielle St John . Ranika Singh . Kelly Jane Thorne
Vanessa West . Shaheeza Haji . Patti Moloney

SARAH VAILL-CIANO & LINDSAY MAE ANDERSON

Contents

Bios

Intro

Hey, Friend!

Right now, you are holding an inspired collection of moments in your hands. There are moments of struggle, ease, alignment, and fear . . . Moments that represented pivotal experiences in the authors' lives. With each page turned, you will be fully immersed in the journey of entrepreneurship. You are holding pure magic.

Can you feel it? #goosebumps

The authors poured out their hearts in these pages. They revealed their struggles with vulnerability. They celebrated their moments of alignment and ease with humility, and they explored those moments of fear with strength, courage, and a deep desire to be better, to do better, and to make an impact in this world!

We ask that you hold space in your heart for the authors as you dive into their journeys because they wrote these chapters with the intention of being of service to YOU, the women of the world who are just getting started.

Just Getting Started in

- Understanding their purpose
- Embodying their core values and beliefs
- Making themselves and their dreams a priority
- Trusting themselves
- Embracing the BOSS that they were born to be!

We honour the women who will eternally live between these pages and in our hearts. We will always be grateful and inspired by the journeys shared here, and we trust deeply that these stories will make an impact on the world as it is today.

By sharing their stories, these women are establishing themselves as leaders in the world of business. They are not Boss Babes or Lady Bosses, they are BOSSES! Plain and simple. They have stepped bravely into this book, facing the fear of being seen and heard in a world full of people who remain in judgment of those who step into the light. They are paving the way. They are sharing their stories of how they got started and how difficult it was so that you can face that fear too. So that you can step in and BE SEEN and HEARD in all your power. In all your authentic expression and all your leadership.

We thank you, from the bottom of our hearts, for supporting these authors by reading and sharing their stories.

Love Always,

Sarah and Lindsay ♥

Invitation

Hey, Future Boss!

As promised, this book has even more depth than each of these incredible stories will offer!

Weaved within these pages are intuitive journal prompts that will challenge you, guide you, and inspire you to lean deeper in your journey today!

We know that you are just getting started, so grab a pen and your journal and let your heart guide you as you answer the questions before and after each chapter.

This invitation allows you to tap in, feel around, and explore the desires that are landing on your heart. Let them take shape on your pages. Let them be born into the Universe today!

GET IT, GIRL!

Reflection Prompt

Why are you here right now, reading this book?

Chapter One

Meet Your Teachers: Friction & Nudge

Lindsay Mae Anderson

She was lying in the yard at her parents' house, pen in hand, journaling everything that came to mind. She allowed the ink to flow and didn't judge anything that she was writing. She landed in her most creative expression and was eager to embrace the depth of possibility.

She felt a deep excitement that she was journaling about writing a book. She was receiving downloads and writing about the profound, sometimes confronting and enlightening messages that she would one day share with the world. She had a vision and a deep inner knowing that her purpose was bigger than the life she was living. She imagined how the book might look, she thought about the energy it would carry, and she wondered what the title would be. The guidance received was "She." Nothing else. Just "She."

She told her best friend, and not long after, her BFF sent her a picture of a book at Chapters, a book called "SHE" that was written

And she knew, in her soul, that it needed to happen.

by the late Kate Spade. Her stomach sank. She felt like her dreams had been ripped away. She was gutted, worried, disappointed, and confused by her inner knowings. Perhaps she wasn't as capable as she had imagined. Perhaps not as creative or insightful either. She didn't want to copyright or plagiarize, and she certainly wasn't familiar with any of the legalities involved. She felt the friction and tossed the idea aside, which, on some level, felt comforting. She no longer needed to achieve this big dream—this outlandish possibility, this far-fetched and incredibly inspiring idea—because someone had already done it. She couldn't possibly compete.

It felt like "She" was a lost cause. It hadn't worked out, despite it feeling right. She pushed it all aside, even her dream of writing a book. Over the next couple of months, though, she continued to feel the nudge toward writing. And she expressed this energy in small, comfortable ways—writing blog entries, journaling, creating social media captions with simple vulnerability. When it felt like it was in alignment, she stepped a bit further into her truth. She submitted an article for a women's empowerment magazine. She signed up for a few podcast opportunities. She dipped her toes, seriously unsure about trusting her worthiness of it all.

She attended a women's summit and listened attentively to a speaker introducing a goal methodology. She was asked to close her eyes and write down the first big goal that came to mind. To her surprise, she wrote "publish the book." She looked up and saw a poster for a new collaborative book. Six months later, her chapter was published, and along with a wonderful client-turned-friend-turned-co-author, she was knee deep in book signings.

Six months later, the friends received a message from Sarah Swain, CEO of the publishing house. Sarah asked if they wanted to co-lead two upcoming books. The books would be part of a series in which she was hoping to shift the focus. It would now be called the "SHE" Series.

There was immediate fear, matched with soul-wrenching excitement. Mouth dropped wide, she could feel the alignment at the core of her being. She had absolutely no idea how it would go, what would come of it, what might be explored and healed. And she knew, in her soul, that it needed to happen. She may have tossed her dream aside, but the Universe had another plan, and it was nudging her toward it.

***

The Universe has a funny way of giving us those little nudges, doesn't it? Some people call it coincidence, other people call it fate. At the end of the day, it doesn't matter what you call it. What matters is that you acknowledge that it's there. And that perhaps it's even had a hand in getting you to this moment, right now. Sometimes, the nudges are subtle. Sometimes, they make us frickin' uncomfortable and demand to be explored.

Isn't that why you're here, right now? Reading this book?

You've received a nudge!

And it's time to trust that nudge, to feel into it and flow with it. To give that nudge a huge HELL YES! It's time to trust that you're here for a BIG reason—one that will not be easily ignored, no matter how hard you might try. No matter what fear holds you back. No matter how long it takes. No matter what limiting beliefs you carry. No matter what society says. No matter what comfort zones you need to smash. No matter how many people have shown up and achieved before you!

***

Entrepreneurship had never actually been a dream of hers; it was not even something that fell on her radar. There had always been an inner knowing that she would help people, though, and that she would lead in some way. This leadership showed up throughout her journey: a deli clerk helping people with their groceries at fourteen, a debt collector helping people manage their finances at twenty-one, a weight-loss coach, a social worker, a doting partner and friend with too much advice to give . . . and the list goes on. She chose a prestigious university fresh out of high school and declared philosophy her major. She had always been intrigued by the expansiveness of people's minds, their reality and existence, their capacities, and most notably, their ego and its conditioning. Psychology classes as well as world religions and creative writing classes spoke deeply to her.

After a failed attempt at said university, and another failed attempt in a college photography program, she was guided toward the weight-loss industry. She was fond of this work—encouraging and coaching people to achieve their goals and maintain their health—but there was a requirement that never sat well with her. There were sales quotas and strategies that left her feeling like she needed to sell products to people in a forceful way. Gross. She could feel the friction this requirement brought up inside her. Despite her natural coaching ability, she was fired because she refused to sell the product. Not surprisingly, the inauthentic sales approach this clinic held was sniffed out, and it was closed not long after. She continued her coaching with a different weight-loss clinic, but the stench of shady sales continued to linger, and it closed too.

She was satisfied with the knowing that she was here to help people, and coaching, encouraging, empowering, and cheerleading felt incredibly natural to her, as was this knowing that she thrived in fluidity and change. She needed space to grow, and she very much dismissed monotonous work and shady sales tactics.

She "randomly" found herself applying to school again. She started her social work program five years out of high school. She graduated with a college diploma and a bachelor's degree from university, both with honours. Social work felt like the most natural thing in the world to her, and it amazed her how she had "stumbled" upon it. She showed up to her studies with excitement and inspiration. While it felt connected with ease, she was still being challenged, which she loved. She piled on psychology classes and creative writing as well, she tutored other students (read: helped them), she maintained a part-time position at a local bar, and she could still pass a social work class without ever even stepping foot in the classroom. During her schooling, she also started to work in the shelter system: shelters for womxn fleeing abusive relationships, shelters for men, shelters for families and for youth who were experiencing homelessness. She was greatly moved by those suffering with mental illness and helping people (surprise!) work toward mental health and wellness.

She started her "dream job" in a mental health organization and quickly moved her way into a case management position. She had a steady income and great benefits. Naturally, climbing the hierarchical ladder was of great importance (read: conditioning), so she was working closely with upper management on specific policy design projects, she was creating incredible relationships with outside agencies and fellow employees, and she was well received by each client in her case files. She embraced the flexibility in schedule and the change of scenery with every call. She had a bright future and had made it clear to her managers and the CEO that she intended to run this organization one day. She would lead . . . she would be the Boss.

She thought she had it made, but it wasn't long before she started suffering from burnout.

In hindsight, she can understand why.

Fast-forward a few years and she'd ditched said "dream job" and ventured out on her own, finding a new, more spiritual and aligned way of being of service (read: helping people).

This vision and deep inner knowing that her purpose was bigger surfaced again. As terrifying as it was, she knew in her gut it had to happen. The consistency of the guidance and the way it was like the Universe just unfolded in front of her, providing little clues as to what steps to take next, was completely immersive and astonishing. She could feel the Universe nudging her toward entrepreneurship. There had been hints all along the way, but it didn't feel feasible. It wasn't the steady, safe, and normal path she was "supposed" to take.

She allowed herself to be nudged, but she received moments of clarity matched with fear, old habits, and feelings of friction. She wasn't the only one who questioned whether she could do it, whether she was ready, and she became obsessed with getting the "right" certifications before she could start this terrifying endeavour. She almost signed up for a program through a local spiritual "school," but after driving all the way there and nearly getting hit by another car, she couldn't even step inside the door. She felt the friction. Whatever it was about this program, it wasn't calling to her the same way other things had recently. It felt forced. It felt like something she "should" be doing, not something that she wanted to do. She drove home, grabbed a journal, and started writing. She felt a deep sense of excitement when she realized she was journaling about programs that she would offer and a soul-led business that would support and empower womxn in their awakening. These were the seeds that planted, and from here, her business centred on intuitive dropdowns and a fierce trust in the Universe. The only certificates she had were her Level I and II Reiki Certifications and, of course, her two social work degrees that she never used again.

One of her first offerings was oracle card readings. She was being nudged to start offering reiki sessions but didn't have the equipment. She made an agreement with Spirit that she would follow their lead and provide reiki sessions if they would help her sell out her card readings, and in turn, she would receive the finances needed to purchase the equipment. Within two weeks, she had the equipment and was starting to offer therapeutic sessions and then mentorship programs. Her offerings continued to expand naturally this way. As she received guidance, she would surrender to the flow and continue to follow the nudges. She would very quickly become an energetic match for the things her heart desired most.

As her business grew rapidly, selling out events and creating new and consistent offerings, she fell in love with her community. Entrepreneurship allowed her to be surrounded by people with similar values, interests, and virtues. People with open minds and humble hearts. People who were committed to doing their healing work and to becoming better versions of themselves. She began embracing her innate intuitive and empathic abilities and stepped into the role of leadership that her soul had been craving. She felt pride in the fact that she had never taken a single business course (unless you count the *Facebook Ads for Dummies* book her mom gave her), and within the first eight months, she blew her annual social work salary right out the window. She was in full rejection of the patriarchal business standards that ran the world: hierarchy, pushy sales, glass ceilings, funnels, codependent marketing strategies, etc. She was simply following the nudges.

Despite the COVID-19 pandemic, her second year in business was a good year. In January 2020 she was nudged to move her business online, so she was already working from this space when lockdowns started in March/April. Her offerings changed, her audience grew, and she embraced this new norm with grace and ease. She rebranded her business several times, inviting the creative dropdowns and expansive energy that rebranding brought with it. She was coasting. And then in 2021, the Universe set her up with a deeper nudge. She was being guided to look with even more refinement at how she could embrace her magic and share it with the world. She was being encouraged to see and express herself even more authentically. She was being challenged to release deeper levels of comfortability in staying safe and small. This nudge came with a layer of intense subconscious healing. She was guided internally to unravel the shameful ways of colonization and racism that consumed her ancestral lineage, all the while not only running her business but processing and taking action as to how she could incorporate these vital awakenings into the consciousness and culture of it. Despite the discomfort she felt, she was inspired, excited, and purposeful!

Again, she thought she had it made . . . but it wasn't long before she started suffering from burnout.

Again.

And now, in hindsight she can understand why.

Both times, burnout for her looked fairly similar. It didn't matter whether she was doing something she truly loved or wasn't. She felt like she was drowning, unable to hold herself above the water, gasping for air, unsure of who to go to for help, or even what kind of help she needed. She would numb out life and emotion with food, with wine, with TV. She would withdraw from people, justifying that she didn't have the space to hold anyone else's energy because, quite frankly, she didn't. She would work too hard, obsess about everything, never make time for things that actually filled her cup. Completely pushing against the grain, adopting as many bad habits as possible, her sense of self slipped into becoming incredibly reliant on impressing and pleasing other people. She was always searching for the light at the end of the tunnel, never allowing herself to reach it, or to be it. She felt disoriented, unmotivated, and generally just discontent and stuck. She felt so heavy and experienced easily her darkest days. And, at the same time, she had convinced herself that her problems weren't "too" terrible.

It's impressive how we can convince ourselves that we're doing okay because we have a few boxes checked. Decent home, decent relationship, decent job, mental health in order on most days of the week . . . check, check, checkity check! All is well . . . until it's not.

In both scenarios, when the Universe was nudging her into another level of alignment, she resisted. Her nervous system shot into high gear and sent her into panic to stay safe and small. She shrank. She numbed out. She distracted herself. She slipped into fear.

Both friction and nudge can be subtle. Both can be loud. And they are both instrumental teachers on our journey.

When we are in friction, we operate from a level of deep conditioning, which is often subconscious. When we surrender to the nudges of the Universe, we make the conscious choice to operate from trust and embody both sacred masculine and sacred feminine energies. It is then when we can create fierce magnetism in our work and home life.

We've signed up for this lifetime, in this exact human form, to create magic. To live a fulfilling life with energetic awareness and wellness, AND we tend to get stuck in our conditioning—what we've learned to be true about the world and the identities we carry here. We learn things like that it's irresponsible to leave one job without having another lined up, that climbing the corporate ladder is the main goal, that it's money in our bank account that proclaims success, not personal fulfillment. We learn that when we feel resistance to something, we should just ignore it, suck it up, and keep going. Push against the grain. We learn to show up as society wants and expects us to, and we prioritize this expectation over how our true, authentic, and heart-driven self wants (or is being nudged) to show up.

When she was burning out, she was operating from conditioning. The relentless thoughts pounded through her head every single day: *You can't do that. That's irresponsible. Just suck it up and keep moving. Work a normal job like everyone else. You'll never be successful if you don't.* Grind, hustle, grind, and hustle again. Friction. And when she realized that she wasn't doing things "by the book," the conditioning got even louder. *How could you ever climb the ladder like this? Who do you think you are?!* For many of us, moving through society today, recognizing and starting to heal our conditioned (or ego) self, we are guided to look at the imbalance that has been created through our patriarchal system. We begin to understand that as part of our conditioning, we have learned to operate from wounded masculine and feminine energies. We've learned to operate from insecurity, from inferiority, and from lack, which are the major contributing factors that keep us unclear on this vision, disconnected from our deep inner knowings, and fearful that our purpose is actually bigger than the life we are currently living.

Wounded masculine energy manifests in different ways, often looking like aggression, a deep desire to control, criticism, and gossip. It can look like fear of failure and getting super absorbed in logic, stuck in the mind and swarmed by thoughts, or never leaning into intuition and feeling. It can feel a lot like inner conflict, which often shows up as mirroring and projection, creating conflict in the world external to us too. For her, the wounded masculine presented itself as hours upon hours upon days and weeks OBSESSING about structure, consistency, and planning in her business. She would beat herself up because her website wasn't clear, and it had taken her years to build it because she was never 100 percent clear on her vision. She felt confused by her own offerings because they didn't fit neatly in a little square systematic box. She was planning courses and never executing them, always getting in her mind and discounting the impact that they could have. She would distract herself with menial tasks. She convinced herself that rebranding and inviting flow into her business was making her appear inconsistent, irresponsible, and unprofessional. She would find herself sometimes in total lack mindset, fearing that there would never be enough: not enough money, not enough clients, not enough opportunity, etc.

When we absorb the wounded masculine energy, we almost always find ourselves with wounded feminine energy too. Wounded feminine energy looks like over providing, compromising our integrity, creating for others rather than from a space of what brings us joy, and (unintentional) codependency. It can leave us drowning in our emotional states, connected primarily to shame and guilt and low self-worth. Her experience looked a lot like self-depreciation, comparison, imposter syndrome . . . very deep limitations bubbling to the surface that forced her to question everything about herself and her business. She would drown in her emotions, completely unable to find a balance between work, joy, and healing. She felt shame and embarrassment for choices that she had made in her business and in her previous career and would try to make up for it by slipping into people-pleasing mode. She would find herself creating from a place of insecurity and the desire to please. She would question whether she was misunderstanding her intuition. She was doing more than what her energetic capacity could handle and wasn't mindful of setting boundaries that would support her.

Living primarily in the unconscious world of conditioning and wounded masculine and feminine, is, and always will be, a perfect recipe for burnout. Friction, friction, friction. However, when we become conscious of our experience, we can recognize that the friction that comes from leaning back toward conditioning and wounded space can be an opportunity to explore the possibility of MORE rather than an opportunity to settle for LESS.

In essence, even the friction that we experience can be considered a nudge.

In essence, even the friction that we experience can be considered a nudge.

When things in your life are out of alignment, the Universe is going to do what it needs to do to bring you back into a space of alignment. A simple metaphor here is about tires. If you've ever been off-roading or in an accident, you know that it's a good idea to get a wheel alignment. This is the process where a mechanic, let's name them Universe, will conduct a process of adjusting vehicle suspension components and the wheels. Universe will ensure that this car leaves the garage in optimal condition so that it has a smooth ride and gets the most of its life. When the car veers off again, Universe is happily waiting to provide another alignment.

When we are feeling this deep-seated friction in our lives, we can trust that the Universe is making us uncomfortable for a reason. Our human selves are being realigned with our soul's callings. Recalibrated. Awakened. Nudged toward the next level of our journey. We are being guided to a deeper space of fulfillment and purpose.

Rather than shrinking, numbing, searching for distractions, or slipping into fear and old habits, we can make the conscious choice to operate from trust, which centres us into a space of balance between both sacred masculine and sacred feminine energies. The sacred masculine is present, aware, structured, decisive, and discerning. Here, we begin to experience this strong sense of clarity of purpose, and we can match it with purposeful action and discipline. We can embrace our sacred feminine, which is this intuitive and compassionate energy that displays this beautiful innocence and excitement in expression. There is creativity and free-flowing trust that is connected deeply to that inner knowing in soul and body.

When she gave herself permission to break through the burnout, she leaned back into her daily routine and started embracing her health. From this space, she was more mindful of her energetic boundaries and how the lifestyle she was living in was contributing greatly to her lack of motivation, joy, and ease. She wakes up earlier and takes moments in her day to sink back into discernment. She creates more space in her calendar for flow. She reads more, makes time for family, and consciously makes the effort to get outside and enjoy the world. She asks for guidance, and she intentionally creates space to allow herself to be nudged and follow through. She leans into flow and gets completely and unapologetically inspired by where it may lead her. With childlike curiosity, she remains open and willing to explore the world in all its beauty.

And then it's not long before she slips back into shrinking, numbing, and entertaining distractions.

And that's okay.

The Universe knows that she is ready for another alignment.

We are a constant work in progress. We will never truly have it figured out. One thing that we can trust, however, is that the Universe is always nudging us toward our highest calling, toward that beautiful vision that feels expansive and scary AF. That's all part of the process—understanding that the times in our lives when we feel most uncomfortable hold just as much magic as the times that we feel most aligned. Entrepreneurship shakes up your life in ways that you will never imagine, and it can create space for more joy, purpose, and alignment than you've ever thought possible! Thinking about, preparing to do it, and starting your entrepreneurship journey is littered with fear, failure, disappointment, hard lessons, and haters.

Trust that this friction has a message.

As does the nudge.

Those big dreams, outlandish possibilities, far-fetched and incredibly inspiring ideas . . . they ARE achievable. Remember, you are here to be amazing. You are here to be happy. You aren't supposed to have it all together, all the time. Your mess is actually your authenticity. Your vulnerability is your value. Your hardest days are the most inspiring, and they carry incredible lessons. Real people need real people to lead them. And you are one of those leaders.

To all the beautiful womxn who have allowed me to hold space for you, thank you!

To all the people who have loved and encouraged me (even if they didn't understand anything I was talking about!), I appreciate you!

And to all the womxn sitting on the fence of their dreams

. . .

The desire is on your heart for a reason.

It is meant to be fulfilled.

It is meant to be born into this world.

Who are you to decide that this world doesn't need your magic?

Lindsay Mae Anderson, Soul Coach and CEO of My CORE Collective

Lindsay Mae Anderson is a self-development, spiritual junkie. She is a Gemini/Capricorn/Leo combo and 6/2 Emotional Mani Gen that claims a serious addiction to sushi and Hallmark movies. Lindsay is a "retired" social worker who began pursuing her soul's purpose after having experienced rock bottom when she lost her job, her relationship, and her sense of self. She is a 3x published author who is committed to sharing her story and inspiring others to speak their truth. Lindsay has been gifted the name "Bridge Between Two Worlds Woman" from an Indigenous medicine woman, and she weaves this name into her soul purpose as she bridges the worlds of spirituality and humanity in all that she does. Lindsay's life work, My CORE Collective, is the invitation your soul has been craving—an invitation for clarity, ownership, remembrance, and embodiment. Her offerings have been described as "nothing short of soul shaking." If you're a part of this girl's circle, you know you will be inspired to live fully and in purpose.

www.mycorecollective.com

"Thinking about, preparing to do it,
and starting your entrepreneurship
journey is littered with fear, failure,
disappointment, hard lessons, and
haters.
Trust that this friction has a message.
As does the nudge.
Those big dreams, outlandish
possibilities, far-fetched and incredibly
inspiring ideas . . . they ARE achievable."

Lindsay Mae Anderson

Reflection Prompt

Where have you experienced friction or resistance in your work and personal life?

Where is the Universe nudging you right now?

Reflection Prompt

How has patriarchy encouraged you to hide your strength as a woman?

Chapter Two

Butterfly Strong: Redefining Strength

Patti Moloney

It was a cold, dreary, grey February day, like most others when you live in Ontario. The kind of day that no matter how many layers you wear, you can't stave off the damp chill from settling into your bones and freezing you from the inside out. With a warm coffee in hand, I was working away at the office. The hum of machinery in the background was white noise that brought a sense of peace and calm to the room, causing my thoughts to stray elsewhere. The words of a friend from earlier in the morning kept replaying in my mind. I could feel them taking root, a new perspective being planted, growing. It was then that I looked up from my work and my thoughts and noticed with new eyes what had been in front of me for years: a hand-painted, teal butterfly on the wall. At that moment, the image meant something altogether different. My thoughts and the butterfly symbol before me merged and transformed into a completely developed concept in my mind. Butterfly Strong was born.

The butterfly has been part of our company's branding since its inception as a symbol of life's special but fleeting moments and as a reminder to be fully present, capturing treasured time with family and friends while we can. Yet on this day, that image took on a whole new meaning. I recognized how fragile a butterfly truly is. With delicate, paper-thin wings, it can be torn in an instant. Despite this fact, the monarch makes a journey of epic proportions, flying thousands of kilometres on its tiny wings, facing the uncertain and often harsh conditions Mother Nature places before it in addition to the endless human-created obstacles and predators. Nonetheless, she endures. She follows her instinct. She perseveres. She is a beautiful contradiction: the coexistence of fragility and strength. While the butterfly might never come to mind as a symbol of strength, it is certainly not weak. Butterflies may be fragile, yes, but they are not weak, as evidenced by their incredible stamina during migration. I'd like to propose a new definition of strength: Butterfly Strong.

There was a clear moment when I decided to commit to contributing to this book, writing this chapter, and sharing the concept of Butterfly Strong in a meaningful way. It was the moment someone described me as not being "tough." One sentence, one small comment out of nowhere, with no context. Seemingly benign. Why did this one tiny word send me into a spiral of silent rage? Because toughness and strength have, for centuries, been defined as the state of being physically strong. And while this definition is definitely one aspect of strength, it is limited and incomplete, a perception that is pervasive and, I feel, harmful. Toughness, grit, and strength are not always outwardly visible. What infuriated me was being summed up by such a limited phrase that ignored all that isn't seen. Sometimes, it's the smallest, simplest moment that trembles your earth and makes you act. Sometimes, it's a moment that catches you off guard, igniting a spark that lights the fire ablaze within you.

Woven into the fabric of our patriarchal society is the perception that strength lies in physical power and the characteristics that align with that, such as assertiveness, decisiveness, and aggressiveness. Certainly, these are incredible strengths to possess. All you kick-butt, awesome women out there who exude these confident qualities, I truly do admire you! This definition of strength, however, is outdated and provides a narrow view of what it is to be strong.

To me, strong looks like the person who wakes up feeling overwhelmed even before she opens her eyes to greet the new day. Her mind is a whirlwind of fears, both real and imaginary. Her overwhelm escalates to a feeling of terror that rests squarely and heavily upon her chest. She is unsure of how she's going to accomplish all she needs to get done that day, unsure of how she can meet all the expectations upon her, from her children, spouse, work, and everything else that pulls her in all directions during the day. The weight of her unreached dreams and the uncertainty of what the future holds tug at her feet, threatening

By reframing how we see ourselves and how we view certain traits, we can turn our weakness into a superpower.

to pull her down into the abyss, threatening to steal her peace and destroy her joy. Nevertheless, she prevails, putting one foot in front of the other, bravely facing the day, meeting the needs of her family, crushing deadlines at work, and making plans for the future. No one she encounters notices the invisible weight of worry she battles with each moment. She conquers a day she felt incapable of handling. She will do the same tomorrow. She is Butterfly Strong.

This person feels sensitive, fragile, vulnerable, and sometimes less capable than others. The fabric of our society tells us that these are feelings of weakness—a perception that we have absorbed and subconsciously believe. But those who make it through days like these have all the power they need to accomplish anything their hearts desire. By reframing how we see ourselves and how we view certain traits, we can turn our weakness into a superpower.

Have you ever felt that being sensitive is a liability? Being empathetic, compassionate, humble, and considerate are the most wonderful of traits—they enable us to feel and care deeply about others. Unfortunately, they also open us up to being hurt, taking things too personally, and caring about what others may think about us. A patriarchal lens frames these traits as being weak and fragile. In reality, the truth is the opposite. These traits are your greatest strengths. In fact, they are the very ones that will save this planet and its people.

In 2020 the world as we know it changed in an instant with the onset of the COVID-19 pandemic. As everyone struggled to adapt, who was it that reached out to ensure seniors were still able to access food and medications? Who checked in with parents who suddenly found themselves working from home with their small children by their sides instead of in school? Who helped communities find a way to celebrate graduates? Who was a beacon of hope to you personally in those days? I'm fairly certain it wasn't aggressive, hard-nosed business leaders. Rather, it was caring neighbours and compassionate citizens who reached out, organized food drives, and started Facebook groups to help people connect with each other. It was an empathetic friend or family member who kept calling and texting to check in on you. In the words of cultural anthropologist Margaret Mead, "Never doubt that a small group of thoughtful, committed citizens can change the world. Indeed, it's the only thing that ever has." These people are the epitome of Butterfly Strong.

Admittedly, I didn't always embrace my own Butterfly Strength. That's putting it mildly. I'm in my forties, I'm a mother of three, a wife, and an entrepreneur, and I'm only just beginning to own who I am. I can admit that, until recently, I actually despised that aspect of myself. I felt weak and vulnerable in comparison to those who were less sensitive. It was others around me who opened my eyes to accepting these gifts. I believe we encounter people and events in our lives for a reason. The veil that was over my eyes began to pull back, revealing people around me who embraced, accepted, and celebrated these gifts.

The more I tried to suppress my emotional, intuitive side, the more emotional I got.

As a business owner and co-founder of DimplesCharms.com, a custom jewellery company, I had the opportunity to be a part of a prestigious Canadian business incubator, and later, an accelerator program. What I noticed among all the amazing, strong, successful female business leaders whom I met, interacted with, read about, or saw in the media was their confidence, assertiveness, decisiveness, even dominance. They were awesome and tough—archetypically strong. It made me wonder, do I have what it takes to succeed if I'm not "all that?" That doubt nagged at me continually.

I tried to demonstrate these qualities more. I worked on being more decisive and assertive. However, as I focused on exuding these traits that I saw in other female leaders, I began to ignore my intuition and suppress my emotional side, believing there was just no place for those "softer" traits in my business life. The more I tried to suppress my emotional, intuitive side, the more emotional I got. I hated it! I couldn't stand that I would cry whenever I was joyful, sad, frustrated, angry, stressed . . . well, pretty much when I felt any which way. It made me feel weak and fragile.

One such moment is forever seared into my memory as mortifying, but in looking back now, I can thankfully laugh out loud at it. It was during an exciting time in our company when we were launching a new technology. It was also a very stressful time. For me, excitement combined with stress is a guaranteed recipe for a show of emotions. We were having a team meeting about the rollout, and my co-founder/husband, Jeff, wasn't able to be there. In my heart, I knew that I would get emotional when the time came to inspire the team through story as we worked through the near-term challenges and tight timelines. I desperately wanted Jeff to chair the meeting so I would be able to escape if/when my emotions became visible (take a bathroom break, etc.). Since that wasn't going to be possible, I vowed to not "feel" that day. Easy-peasy, brilliant solution . . . except for the fact that it didn't work.

In the middle of the meeting, during a passionate moment of inspiration, tears just started rolling down my face. I didn't skip a beat in what I was saying, and I tried to ignore the fact that they were there. Of course, people noticed, and I remember saying, "Yes, these are tears, but it's all okay. It doesn't actually mean anything. I'm just excited. Ignore them. Really. I mean it. Pretend they aren't there." The meeting continued with spirited team discussion as planned. Afterward, I felt pretty embarrassed. I tried instead to be proud of myself for acknowledging the tears but not letting them derail me. I felt like it went okay. That is, until the next day.

The next day, two team members arrived separately with a small gift for me. It's worth noting that at the time, I was the only female on this tiny team, so two members actually represented a third of the group. One brought me a chocolate bar and the other brought me a playlist. I should have felt loved and cared for. I should have recognized the Butterfly Strength in each of these men who were so thoughtful and considerate. I should have felt honoured and graciously accepted their acts of kindness. I should have. Except, I was MORTIFIED. Mortified is really the only way to describe how I felt. I said thank you, but I slunk away horrified. They were supposed to ignore the tears! Why did the tears have to mean anything? I suddenly felt that showing emotion was wrong. I deeply regretted it and again despised my nature of being "a softie."

Looking back now, I know that was a misconception. From my perspective now, I know these team members just wanted to demonstrate their understanding of my feelings. But at the time, that's not how I perceived the situation. To me, it was another example of how I was too emotional to be a leader.

One day, a friend and business associate told me, "Patti, that's your superpower!"

"What?"

"Your superpower. You feel. The world beats the heart out of most people. The fact that you still feel so much, that is a superpower. The world needs more people with heart. Embrace it!"

"What?" I cannot describe the fury her statement evoked in me. It's funny to me now, but at the time, I was infuriated. Angry to . . . you guessed it . . . tears. "What kind of lame superpower is that? I actually can't stand that part of me! Superpower? [Insert swear words here.] If I had a superpower, it would be teleporting! [Insert more profanity here.]" She waved and exited with a smile, which, of course, enraged me.

Every time I saw her after that, she said the same thing. I know to examine my feelings when my reaction to something is more extreme than the event itself calls for. I asked myself, "Why does the idea of me having heart and being sensitive elicit such anger in me?" I realized that I believed subconsciously what for centuries has been the dominant paradigm of our culture: that emotion, sensitivity, and vulnerability, all traits considered "feminine" and even nurturing, are associated with weakness. The single role that stereotypically embodies these traits is motherhood. In politics, history, business, and much of mass media and entertainment until recently, feminine and nurturing characteristics have been equated with weakness. Yet, what position in this world is more powerful than motherhood? Honestly, I can't think of one.

The more I mulled this thought over, the more I came to value such characteristics. My perspective shifted as I challenged my own interpretation of what strength really was. Eventually, my attitude softened, and when I next heard about my so-called superpower, I thought, *What if she isn't totally wrong? In fact, what if she's right?*

It was then that I looked up from my work and saw the teal butterfly painted on our office wall. The veil before my eyes had been pulled back and a new strength was born in me. Rather than trying to rid myself of my weaknesses, my perspective began to change and I could see clearly the utter strength that existed in what I had once deemed as weaknesses. A perspective shift occurred, setting my world back on the axis it was always meant to be on.

Interestingly, when I look back at any of the make-or-break moments in our business, times where crucial decisions were made (whether or not we were conscious of their importance at the time), the decisions that moved us forward and got us through were those that were determined by intuition, gut feeling, and emotion. Each and every one.

Two such occasions occurred when we were presented with an opportunity for a partnership. Twice, years apart from each other, we were on the verge of entering a partnership. Both occasions signified a very important decision and major change for our company. On paper, all the standard indicators looked great. But I had an unrelenting feeling that things just wouldn't go well. It was more than just nervousness over a change; it was a gut instinct. Each time, I ignored it and ignored it, figuring it was just nerves, until I almost became physically ill. Finally, I confessed this gut feeling to my husband and business partner, Jeff. "We need to listen to your gut, Patti. It has never misled us," he said with determination. Suffice it to say, we didn't go through with either partnership, and in both cases, we avoided a near disaster each time. I'm not kidding. Our company wouldn't exist today if we had partnered either time. These experiences taught me that staying in tune with your intuition is as important in business as tracking KPIs and knowing financials. Eventually, the right partnership came along, and I knew it without a doubt.

Ironically, I thought it was a liability to permit my "softer side" to have a seat at the table in my business, when in fact, my subtle strengths have been the keys to my success. In striving to be what I thought I should be—what I thought would make me successful and strong—the weaker I became. Leaning into my own wisdom and allowing my emotional intelligence to guide me is where my strength had been all along.

It was during the pandemic that Butterfly Strong took form, close on the heels of first admitting to my "superpower." During daily walks/runs over the years with my friend and neighbour, we'd often find ourselves discussing the rewards and frustrations of being sensitive. We'd talk passionately about the misconception that strong is the demonstration of

I was more fearful than confident, to be honest. My mantra in those moments is "Doubt and do it anyway," and I usually surprise myself with the results.

decisive confidence and physical strength. This concept was never more obvious or evident to me than during the pandemic, when the gifts of resilience, service, humility, perseverance, gentle courage, and compassion sustained humanity.

Owning a jewellery company, of course, fuelled me to create a piece of jewellery to embody the notion of Butterfly Strong. I envisioned a talisman, a symbol and constant reminder of one's inner truth and sometimes fragile but ever-remaining strength. We developed the concept for a Butterfly Strong necklace based on the butterfly on the wall of our shop. Each necklace would come with a card printed on seed paper that grows flowers to attract butterflies. On the card, a message would read: "This necklace is a celebration of subtle strengths that are often overlooked and undervalued. However, with them we make the world a better place. Sensitivity. Compassion. Empathy. Vulnerability. You are blessed with these characteristics. They are gifts that some may see as weaknesses. I want you to know that they are your greatest strengths! Wear this necklace and remember . . . You make the world a better place!" On the reverse it says, "I admire [and a place to write a name] because [with a place to write an explanation]. Plant this card and watch this movement grow."

We weren't sure how it would "fly," so before even committing to making them, we set a minimum order number before actually launching the product. If we didn't meet the minimum order, then we'd know the concept wasn't resonating with people. Do you know that special kind of terror you feel when you are about to put something that is personally meaningful to you out into the world? It's a tug of war as you vacillate between excitement to move forward and the primal instinct to retreat and abandon the idea. Like the caterpillar who sheds its skin as it grows to a new size and capability, accepting our gifts and moving forward with our inspired ideas requires us to shed old limitations and self-perceptions to grow into a new version of ourselves.

I was more fearful than confident, to be honest. My mantra in those moments is "Doubt and do it anyway," and I usually surprise myself with the results. It might sound silly that launching a product with a personal message was any kind of a challenge but making a personal idea public and open to judgment, scrutiny—and worse, the possibility of failing if it doesn't resonate with anyone—feels scary. I was on a mission to change the traditional perception of strength and to empower people who have felt weak for much of their lives based on these traditional notions. To my surprise and delight, the message resonated deeply!

People were drawn to the idea, wanting to empower those with gentle courage, those who act in service, and those who persevere and are resilient even when they feel fragile. Butterfly Strong had wings!

I made an interesting and important discovery through the necklace project. I found that some people with whom the message resonated strongly were people I did not expect. In fact, some of the "toughest" people I know, in the traditional sense of the word, were huge fans of the concept and related to it completely. I humbly came to understand that each and every single human on this planet feels weak and vulnerable at times. Everyone can relate to feeling fragile on the inside while carrying out normal, everyday life outwardly. Sometimes, the most brazen persona or dominant character is just that: a persona—a coping mechanism portrayed to shield one's inner tenderness. This isn't news, I know. I had just never witnessed someone connecting with this type of message who seems so indomitable from an outsider's view. It's a reminder that nothing is as it seems, and we are all more alike than we realize.

People appreciate the delicate beauty and flight of the butterfly, but few acknowledge the transformational journey that leads to the emergence of this winged creation from its cocoon. It must crawl before it can soar. Let's acknowledge our quiet, courageous warriors whose subtle traits of sensitivity, vulnerability, compassion, and empathy are often overlooked. The strongest women we know survive and thrive by drawing upon their inner wisdom, their personal strength, and their perseverance time and again. Resilient fragility. Fragile enough to feel and to care combined with the courage to lean into those feelings and take action.

My mistake was believing that strength meant always being confident and assured and never doubting decisions. Life and perspective have shown me that strength is, in fact, having doubts and fears but not letting them prevent you from taking action. Doubt and do it anyway. Fear and fail forward. Strength follows action, especially a series of imperfect actions. Do this often enough and you'll find a new strength and confidence that you didn't see coming. It emerges when you act, regardless of your fears. In the words of Bruce Lee, "Courage is not the absence of fear, it is the ability to act in the presence of fear."

Do you know what a flock of butterflies is called? I remember wondering about it and being surprised and delighted by the answer when I discovered it. A kaleidoscope! To me, it's the perfect metaphor. A kaleidoscope reveals to its viewers ever-changing perspectives through a vibrant and colourful lens with each slight movement. As humans, we have the exceptional gift of being able to change our perspective with the slightest shift, should we dare to. My hope is that in reading this brief story, your kaleidoscope has shifted and your perspective on strength has broadened. May you still see strength as heroic, but acknowledge that it is often barely visible, just like the almost imperceptible vibration of a butterfly's wings. As more humans accept and activate their subtle strengths and empower others to do so as well, the vibration becomes a powerful beat like that of a chorus of hearts joining together in song.

I am so grateful for a life filled with Encouragers. Find yourself some because they truly are the best type of people with whom to surround yourself. Andrea, my Butterfly Strong sister and my favourite part of any day! Sarah, the first to lift the veil. I can be infuriated by you and love you for it at the same time—a sign of true friendship. Kerry, the best at reminding me to not give a sh*t about dumb stuff or what people think. Julie, for the last mile. Sometimes, you need a final nudge to take the plunge. Jeff, for a lifetime of encouragement for which I can't thank you enough. Your belief in me will never cease to amaze me. You're the best partner I could ask for on this adventure called life.

Patti Moloney is a wife, mother of three, and an elementary teacher turned entrepreneur. She is co-founder of DimplesCharms.com, a successful custom jewellery company, alongside her husband. She exchanged security and summers off for the roller coaster of entrepreneurialism and wouldn't have it any other way. Patti has written for industry publications, been featured on popular podcasts, radio and television, and has inspired people through courses and speaking engagements on topics of entrepreneurialism and Butterfly Strong.

For a long time, Patti believed that being sensitive was a liability until she realized that true strength is found in embracing your fragility and softheartedness. Patti employs her master's degree in Counselling Psychology to build community and leadership skills through Butterfly Strong, showing people how to lean into their subtle strengths, reframe what they believe are weaknesses, and live and lead with heart to build a stronger world. This concept transforms individuals and institutions alike. Join the Butterfly Strong movement yourself! Visit https://dimplescharms.com/butterfly-strong to learn more about where and how to connect.

IG @dimplescharms

"People appreciate the delicate beauty and flight of the butterfly, but few acknowledge the transformational journey that leads to the emergence of this winged creation from its cocoon. It must crawl before it can soar. Let's acknowledge our quiet, courageous warriors whose subtle traits of sensitivity, vulnerability, compassion, and empathy are often overlooked."

Patti Moloney

Reflection Prompt

What are some of your most subtle, overlooked traits? How might these traits serve a powerful purpose in your business?

Reflection Prompt

What was "that moment" in your life that forced a pivot or a full-fledged detour and brought you to where you are today?

Chapter Three

Pivoting Like a Boss

Shaheeza Haji

There are 7.9 billion people out there with whom we share this beautiful earth, and every single one of them is going through, has gone through, or will go through their own struggles while navigating their own paths. Being real about our struggle doesn't make us weak, it makes us human. And I have learned to be unapologetically authentic about mine.

Back in 2013 at the tender age of twenty-seven, I had my entire life meticulously planned out. I was a physiotherapist who would work hard for a few years, learn as many skills as possible, make as many connections as I could, and then open a freaking empire of rehabilitation clinics of my own. I made it my self-imposed goal to dominate the rehabilitation medicine world, envisioning a string of clinics popping up across Alberta. In my mind, nothing could stop me or slow me down.

September 2013

After years of grinding through my university career to obtain a bachelor's and master's degree and a couple of subsequent entry-level physiotherapy positions, I finally landed that coveted downtown Toronto dream job. No wait. This was better! Situated within walking distance from the Rogers Centre, home to the Toronto Blue Jays, as well as the Air Canada Centre, home to the Toronto Maple Leafs and Toronto Raptors, I was finally in the big leagues! It wasn't just a killer downtown gig, I was among the greats! I couldn't help but let this elation seep through in every conversation I had over those next few weeks, telling anyone who would listen about all I would learn through this amazing experience.

November 27, 2013

Things were fantastic! I had already had the opportunity to meet multiple high-level office executives and professional athletes. I simply adored treating this downtown demographic! To help fit the part, for the first time in years, I spent the evening splurging on a couple of new work outfits. It felt so surreal to leave work, walk a few minutes, and be inside the legendary Eaton Centre. As I left with a surplus of bags, my cousin, who also happened to be my roommate, popped up as an incoming call on my phone. I vividly remember laughing about the over-the-top purchases I had just made as I walked toward the exit. Yeah, some purchases were probably unnecessary, but I had finally earned the opportunity to spoil myself! Life was good, and all was going according to plan.

November 28, 2013

On that crisp November morning, the sun seeped in through my floor-to-ceiling windows of my downtown Toronto loft, signalling the start of my day. I jumped out of bed and began my daily morning routine without thought, just as I had repeated each morning for years. But on this day, I put on a brand-new sweater and a brand-new pair of pants! I grabbed my coffee and walked out the door toward the streetcar that had taken me to work every day for the past two months. I didn't know it, but by the time I would return home, my life would be turned upside down.

3:30 p.m.

I had been working with a patient on a "hi-lo" bed—one of those ergonomically friendly medical beds that moves up and down, aimed at preventing injuries to the therapist. I had treated patients on these beds hundreds of times before. But on this particular day, things didn't go as smoothly as they had every other time in the past.

The treatment session started out as they usually do—an exchange of pleasantries followed by the treatment itself: a combination of hands-on manual therapy and modalities such as dry-needling, education, and exercises. I recall having the "hi-lo" bed in a heightened position as I demonstrated a new exercise program, and I followed it up by informing my patient that I would be lowering the bed so that he could safely move from it to perform the prescribed exercises. However, when I stepped on the pedal, the bed did not budge, leaving my patient in a heightened position. Thinking that the cord had simply come loose from the socket, I bent under the bed to confirm. What happened next is a bit of a blur.

All I can really remember is feeling a sudden jolt of energy throwing me backward and turning my head toward the left—the direction of my patient. After that, I blacked out. The next thing I recall is having my right hand on the bed, struggling to get myself to my feet, unsure as to why I was on the ground. As I attempted to stand, I felt Bambi-esque. My limbs felt weak and jelly-like. My body felt depleted and winded. I remember feeling an intense pressure in my head, seeing stars, and having tunnel vision; I knew things were happening around me, but I could only process muffled murmuring as if my head were under water. Everything felt as if it were occurring in slow motion.

I recall being extremely confused about what had happened, but being the type A person that I was, I remember trying to brush it off and push through for my patient. Immediately, he told me to stop. He asked me if I knew what had happened, to which I had no answer. He, being an electrical engineer, pointed out a penny-sized entrance wound on my hand and explained that I had been electrocuted. He then showed me a completely severed cord, holding up the end that should have been attached to both the bed and the socket.

Shortly after, I started to experience an immense headache, and I was having an incredibly difficult time concentrating. I began having chest pains and an intense ringing in my right ear. I can't remember much more than bits and pieces.

5:00 p.m.

I was taken to the emergency department where a number of tests were carried out. I was told that I had undergone some major shock (apparently electricity will do that!), and that if symptoms worsened, to come right back. Over the next seventy-two hours, inflammation set in, and my symptoms continued to worsen. I experienced excruciating neck and arm pain. I developed an incredible sensitivity to sound and light. I was lethargic, I was extremely nauseated and dizzy, and I had a throbbing headache unlike any I had ever experienced before.

December 1, 2013

It wasn't until December 1, 2013, that my symptoms really started to worry those around me. I had developed a stutter when I talked, and my memory and concentration were declining. I recall taking approximately eight hours to watch a ninety-minute movie because I could not remember what was happening throughout, which forced me to continually stop, rewind, and rewatch. Doing so worried me to no end, since I could previously multi-task without a problem: I could watch movies while studying and engaging in conversation, all while balancing a bowl on my head (okay, maybe not that last part, but you know what I mean). Movies aside, it was so frustrating to experience wanting to get a thought out but not having my mouth cooperate, or worse, forgetting the thought before it even left my mouth.

People around me would ask me questions, to which I could not remember answers, and I was uber annoyed with the frequency with which I would have to ask for things to be repeated. I became agitated and irritated easily. I was unable to hold something as simple as a knife without dropping it, feeling as though I had lost the strength as well as the control of my upper extremity. And my lower extremities were not left out of the picture. I couldn't keep my legs still in bed, as they developed an incredibly irritating and uncontrollable twitch and tremor that would creep in just as I was getting comfortable or falling asleep. I was breaking down emotionally, crying for no explainable reason. I was terrified; what was happening to my body? Why couldn't I maintain a conversation? Why couldn't I think straight? Why was I in so much damn pain? So, I was taken back to the emergency department.

At the hospital, the doctor attending to me provided me with an expedited referral to the head injury clinic, believing that I had suffered an "electrical concussion," for lack of better terminology. What the hell did that even mean? Was my injury really so unusual that he had to preface his diagnosis with "it presents like a concussion, but it's not the same mechanism one would typically find themselves concussed by, but you were also electrocuted, so there's that . . ." or something along those lines?

Approximately ten bedridden days later, I was seen at the clinic and diagnosed with a diffuse traumatic brain injury. The thought process was that the electrical current may have travelled the path of least resistance: from my hand, up through my nervous system toward my brain. Because there was no exit wound, the current would have essentially exploded within the confined space of my skull, creating micro-trauma to different areas of the brain tissue. I also had a herniated jaw that required surgery and third-degree whiplash with associated neurological damage.

Safe to say, the life path I had been carefully constructing was uprooted within the course of a few seconds by the path of least resistance.

For the first time in a decade, I was required to move back home to the

I had always been the independent, type A, goal-oriented one . . .

care of my family at the age of twenty-seven. I said it was tender before, but let's be real. Age twenty-seven is not when someone wants to be moving back home after they've gotten used to independent living throughout the previous decade! The next year of my life consisted of uncertainty, pain, rehab/recovery, a loss of independence, a loss of confidence, mental health struggles, and a lot of time spent in my bed, alone in the dark.

Increasingly frustrated with my situation as the months went by, I found myself asking the typical "why me?" questions one asks when they go through a life-changing experience. I had always been the independent, type A, goal-oriented one, but now I had to watch from the sidelines as all my peers continued to trek forward with their lives while mine was at a standstill. Because many of my inner circle could not understand how altered my life was—or simply didn't care—and because I found it increasingly difficult to relate to many of these people because I could no longer partake in most of the activities I had previously shared with them, I found myself losing a lot of my friends. I still vividly remember the harsh words coming out of an ex-partner's mouth as he broke up with me at the suggestion of his father who had educated him on how miserable his life would be if having to care for "a handicapped person." I found myself anxious and depressed about the state of my stalled life, obsessively comparing it to the one I had envisioned previously. I was unable to accept or recognize what my life had been forced to become.

Instead of accepting my situation and new set of limitations, I frustratedly found a solution that would allow me to continue to be the person I had known for twenty-seven years: pushing myself to my limits and overmedicating just to get by. At the height of it, I was downing twenty-two different pills a day. One in particular came with warnings to not consume more than two within a forty-eight-hour time span. But go-big-or-go-home me? I often took up to six within twenty-four hours. Yep, I mastered a cycle of ignoring my body's warning signs (a.k.a. pain), popped a few pills instead, and put on a happy face. This cycle allowed me to push myself beyond my limits in order to keep up with my peers and the societal definitions of what a twenty-seven-year-old "should" be doing, only to come home, take more medication, and be in severe pain and agony. Yeah, I mastered pretending to be happy to give myself a few hours of pleasure with my friends, then returned home to the closed doors of hell where I was isolated and alone. Serotonin syndrome, liver damage, GI issues, mental health struggles, and multiple withdrawal symptoms proved that this lifestyle was not a viable long-term option. My doctor laid it out bluntly for me: If I continued along this path, death was a real option. I was so focused on getting back to the person I had known for the previous years of my life, not realizing that the "old me" had already died as the electricity ran through my body.

One day along this journey I had an epiphany. As much as my situation dampened my spirits, as much pain as I was in, and as derailed as my perfectly planned out life had become, I STILL had it much better than most people out there. Of course, I hated being in pain every day, but I was lucky enough to have access to endless supplies of medication and an extensive health care team spanning multiple cities at my fingertips. I began to think of how when symptoms got really bad and all I wanted was to be alone in the darkness of my room and the comfort of my bed, I was able to do so. I began to think of how someone somewhere else in the world was likely struggling with a far worse situation and was doing so with far less. And I began to dive into a deep hole of pondering how I had no real explanation for it.

Why is it that some people seemingly have much greater struggles than others? Why is it that some people seem to get the short end of the stick in life? And why do some people seem as though they have it all? I could have had this same incident occur in a third world country. Or I could have had this same incident occur without a support system. But for unexplainable reasons, I was placed in this time and space with these sets of circumstances. I began to acknowledge that while I had a plan for my life, life had a bigger plan for me.

With this epiphany, I revamped my mindset: I could sit there and feel pity about my situation, or I could recognize that I was truly blessed, despite my hardship. Author Mark Manson explains, "We all get dealt cards. Some of us get better cards than others. And while it's easy to get hung up on our cards, and feel we got screwed over, the real game lies in the choices we make with those cards, the risks we decide to take, and the consequences we choose to live with. People who consistently make the best choices in the situations they're given are the ones who eventually come out ahead in poker, just as in life. And it's not necessarily the people with the best cards."

I chose the latter, and this moment became the most fundamental shift in my life to date, changing me from someone who merely went through the motions of life on a day-to-day basis to someone who now lives each day with purpose. I began to shift my focus away from complaining about how things "should" have played out and started to embrace how things *were* playing out. I committed myself to finding the purpose and meaning behind my experience because there had to be something to learn from it. And what I learned was substantial; we are all put on this earth with our own unique higher purpose, potential, strengths, weaknesses, and struggles. Our paths are not meant to be identical. If we all went through life in the same manner, we would never have the opportunity to learn from one another and grow in humanity.

Equipped with this mentality, I began to remind myself of all the blessings I did have: I came to be grateful that I still had an education;

I still possessed the skills of leadership and confidence; I had access to technology and the tools to both increase and share my knowledge. And it became clear to me that it was my duty to use my abundances in these areas to help those who may not have had access to the same. My years of education were no longer just for me to have access to monetary gains. Instead, I now began to realize that I was blessed with the opportunities, grit, and determination to reach my fullest potential so that I could then use those skills to help empower others to achieve theirs, and I came to believe that if we all do the same collectively, we can leave the world a better place.

In the months leading up to this aha moment, I was depressed about my life plan being snatched away from me. But after this moment, I came to dedicate my energy to other areas. I realized from my near-death experience that life is not to be taken for granted—it's too damn short. For too many years prior to my incident, I had let precious time waste away. But I now knew that I was put here for a reason. Having previously felt heavy, lonely, disconnected, and hopeless, this realization brought me to a space of hope and optimism. In this moment, I could feel this lightness from the newfound acceptance take over me.

Firstly, volunteering became a prominent part of my life. Helping to serve others without any monetary motivation backing it continues to fuel me with a profound sense of purpose. Most of my volunteer work to date centres around consultation toward various health boards.

However, my goal is to one day head to Africa, the birthplace of my parents. It is my hope to dedicate my time and resources to those living in poverty there, helping them reach their fullest potential despite life handing them a difficult card.

Secondly, I also shifted gears and began to teach, acting as a head of curriculum development for a physiotherapy assistant program at a local college. I had never seen myself teaching before, but I decided to give it a shot when I realized that the physically demanding nature of being a physiotherapist was no longer in my cards, as the pain exacerbations were too frequent and severe to sustain a career in this manner long term. While instructing was not what I had initially set out to do, it was incredibly rewarding to be able to impart my knowledge on others, and even more humbling to have students later approach me, notifying me of how I played a part in changing their lives. One such example is that of a student who had been homeless earlier in life. Upon completing the diploma program, she was able to utilize the knowledge learned to secure gainful employment opportunities of her own. Knowing that I played a card in this hand fuels me to want to continue.

But I still had a burning inside of me, telling me that I had to use my purpose in a much bigger way before I was gone. I had to make an impact on the world in a larger way. I had to leave behind a legacy. Teaching and volunteering are and will continue to be huge parts of my life, but I needed to use my own pain to help others who were also living in pain. If I have to chronically experience pain for the rest of my days, then I need to find purpose behind its existence in my life.

Thinking in this way, I couldn't help but continually return to my lifelong dream of opening a clinic. I wanted to help as many people suffering from pain as I could; plus, being a persistent sufferer of chronic pain would make me an ideal candidate because I could empathize with my patients. I wanted to provide a beacon of hope to those who had lost hope and were feeling depressed about living in a state of pain like had been the case for me. But as excited as I was by this idea, I was also deflated by these thoughts. My body simply could not keep up with the physically demanding nature of working as a physiotherapist. Prior to my electrocution, I had gotten used to treating twenty to thirty patients a day, but my resultant chronic pain and fatigue would simply not allow for that anymore. In fact, over more recent years, I had attempted to work again as a physiotherapist, but it was always cut short due to my being in excruciating pain, leading to the dangerous cycle of overmedicating I had gotten to know far too well.

In all truth, the extent of pain and resultant unhappiness from pushing myself to get back to treating patients had led to a dark period of my life where I questioned the point of living. What was the point of pushing myself to do the job I loved when it no longer brought me happiness but rather pain, resentment, and unhappiness? What was the point of living a life where I went to work, only to exacerbate my symptoms, come home and overmedicate, then wake up and do it all again the next day?

There had to be another way. I began to shift my vision, accepting that if I were to venture down this path, I likely wouldn't be able to treat patients in the way I had previously done so. Things would have to look vastly different than they may have looked had I not sustained the injuries I had. It was not easy to accept this fact, but I held onto the belief that I could still make an impact.

So, I decided to dive into clinic ownership while taking a huge step back from actively treating patients. (I now only treat patients once a week.) It was difficult to accept a huge loss in potential income from having to hire other therapists to perform the treatments that I initially envisioned myself being able to do on my own. But overseeing all areas of clinical operations without being tied up with patient care has allowed me to offer gainful employment to a team of ten individuals to date! Additionally, I have been able to use my teaching skills to provide mentorship to my young team that often approaches me for assistance and guidance. My hope is to empower them to become the best versions of themselves as therapists and humans.

In regard to patient care, I have created a team-based approach in which I act as case manager and oversee all treatment plans. In doing so, I have been able to act as a liaison, advocating for patients of the clinic by referring them to other health care providers whom I have built sound relationships with, fighting for additional treatments from insurance providers, and building a clinic where patients are able to have all aspects of their rehabilitation addressed under one roof. In a nutshell, I am building what I wish had existed when I was going through the rehab process. It has been extremely humbling to use my knowledge in the area of health care as well as the empathy I gained from my own experience to assist patients in navigating their recovery.

Additionally, an area I have naturally become very passionate about is concussions, which is still in its infancy within the medical community. As such, I began consuming myself with literature and research, initially as an effort to decrease my reliance on over-consuming medication, hoping to implement some of the findings I came across. Engrossed by the research, I underwent continued education and became certified in the assessment, treatment, and management of concussions. Today, my sole area of patient care revolves around concussions, as I am determined to help this patient population cope with this often-invisible injury. This journey has been immensely powerful for me, as my experience of continued symptoms allows me to be ever empathetic with my patients, building a connection unlike most others. Although we learned about pain in school, it's tough to fully understand a patient's struggles unless you have also walked in their shoes.

And in line with my wish to leave the world a better place than when I entered, owning a clinic has allowed me to set up endeavours that I hold near and dear to my heart, one of which is our initiative to plant a tree back into the earth for every new patient into the clinic. Why trees? Well, trees help clean the air we breathe by absorbing harmful pollutants such as nitrogen oxides, ozone, and carbons from the atmosphere, and they release clean oxygen back in. In fact, one mature tree can provide the daily oxygen for up to four people and can absorb more than forty-eight pounds of carbon dioxide a year! Although we have only been open for about a year, we have planted enough trees to provide the daily oxygen for 3,000 individuals and the equivalent of 35,000 pounds of carbon dioxide absorption!

Taken together, I now feel it is my life's purpose to contribute as much as I possibly can to the understanding and continued knowledge around the area of concussions, to not only help with treatment but to also empower my patients with the education and tools to manage their symptoms so they can, in turn, live their most optimal lives. I want to use my time, knowledge, and resources to help others reach their fullest potential, and to leave the world a better place than it was when I entered. And because I am human, I often find myself forgetting these

I want to use my time, knowledge, and resources to help others reach their fullest potential . . .

lessons. But every time I have a migraine or debilitating pain now, yes, a part of me may be sad or frustrated, but a bigger part of me tells me that the pain is simply a reminder to not lose sight of the bigger picture.

Life has a hell of a way of teaching us the lessons that point us toward our deeper purpose. My experience has taught me that with every proverbial storm that confronts our journey, we may face darkness, pain, loss, damage, and setbacks that rattle us to our core. But I am also now confident that every storm is merely wetting the soil to set the stage for beautiful inner growth. We were all put in this time and space with purpose, so grow, baby, grow!

Shaheeza Haji is a health care professional, having graduated with a Bachelor of Arts from the University of Alberta in 2009, followed by a Master of Physiotherapy from the University of Western Ontario in 2011. Being a staunch believer in "exercise is medicine," Shaheeza attained her Certified Strength and Conditioning Specialist status through the National Strength and Conditioning Association in 2013.

At the end of that same year, Shaheeza was involved in a major life-altering, freak incident, leaving her to live with chronic pain and health conditions. She now uses her knowledge and personal experience gained from this incident to empathize with those she meets, encouraging everyone to live life according to their fullest potential. Shaheeza also has a drive for entrepreneurship, being the CEO of Running Shoe Inc., directing both Running Shoe Restorative Healthcare and the Calgary Concussion Centre.

When not at the clinic, Shaheeza is happiest on a mountain or a body of water. When unable to be there, she can be found on a longboard, shooting hoops, or attempting to golf. She is an avid basketball fan, a non-fiction reader, and a lover of travel.

www.runningshoehealth.com

IG @Runningshoe_Restorativehealth

"It became clear to me that it was my duty to use my abundances in these areas to help those who may not have had access to the same."

Shaheeza Haji

Reflection Prompt

In what ways has a pivot (or detour) brought you to a place of understanding your duty?
What abundances do you have access to that you can use to support others?

Reflection Prompt

What conditions and limiting beliefs have you encountered that have been placed on you in the working world?

Are you "too much" of something or "not enough" of something else to be considered "successful" in this society?

Chapter Four

Unapologetically Moi

Aisha Saintiche

Have you ever taken a moment to sit back and think about your life journey and how you got to where you are at this moment? Whether in the place you desire to be or not, how many of us pause, and I mean really pause and think about the ups and downs, challenges and triumphs, and hardships and revelations that have become our personal tapestry?

In June 2020 I was given an amazing opportunity to be a keynote speaker at a conference called "Conversation 2021." The purpose of the event was to gather leaders and athletes from across Canada and the Pan Am Games who were prepared to be game changers when it came to women and sports. It was an opportunity of a lifetime, and while I nearly shit my pants when it came time to execute, I am convinced that our best work comes from nerves (definitely NOT a scientific fact, but seeing as it has always been my experience, Imma claim it as fact!). As is customary when you are the keynote speaker and MC for the event, your bio about all your achievements and accomplishments are read out loud ('cause that's also not anxiety provoking, right?). As she talked and provided details about my personal and professional experience, my contribution to the coaching world, and my volunteering stints that actually fuelled my passion for all things connected to people and empowerment, for a split second I thought to myself, *Wouldn't it be amazing to meet this woman they are speaking about?* And then I remembered they were talking about me!

As the words rolled off my co-lead's tongue, I can't lie—I was overwhelmed with pride, and not because I was the top of the top but because I knew all that I had sacrificed, all that I had risked, all that I had doubted, and all that I triumphed and thrived through to have achieved these accolades. You know, ladies, we don't spend FAR enough time shining a light on ourselves. We do and accomplish so much, but because we think what we are doing is only about "keeping up," we don't honour the fact that we are growing, evolving, and becoming. Lord KNOWS that at one time in my life I had fallen into that abyss of "I need to do more."

You see, over the course of my life, I, like many of you, have done what I have been conditioned or expected to do when it came to personal and professional growth. I went to school, got various certifications and degrees, got a good job, got married, bought a house, had kids

Our personal responsibility, our act of self-love and self-preservation is to let those around us know that we are our priority.

(three to be exact), and lived a life that provided me with personal contentment. In search of nothing more than the life I had created and surviving almost two years of COVID-19 fairly unscathed, I counted my lucky stars that I still had all the things that meant the most to me.

Life as we know it may be one of the most unpredictable things in this world. Sure, we plan, prepare, create contingency plans—heck, some of us may even be able to prevent shit from happening—but the truth is every single day that we open our eyes to another day, we don't actually know what we are about to face. As someone who considers herself to be a planner and a lover of all things organization (that can also be placed into a spreadsheet or chart—and that is not an exaggeration), I want to share a story about stepping out of your comfort zone and stepping into your actual power source that comes from just living authentically and unapologetically.

As a certified health coach, something I constantly tell my clients, especially women, is to stop waiting for someone in your life to take notice of all the shit you do and queue you into your self-care! Girl, ain't no one got that kind of time to take note of ALLLLLLLLL that you do, and yet we expect those around us to create time for us to break. Let me ask you, how's that working for you? Our personal responsibility, our act of self-love and self-preservation is to let those around us know that we are our priority. The same concept applies to your greatness. Why are you undermining your greatness by "waiting" for your business, or any personal achievement for that matter, to be complete? Don't you know starting something new, taking on a project or challenge is the ACTUAL achievement? Making a commitment to personal evolution is so worthy of celebration that if I could figure out how to put sound to this statement, you would hear me yell, "YOU ARE WORTHY OF CELEBRATION!"

Now, the story I am about to share will not be the reality for all, but the takeaway I hope you gain from it is that no one should queue you into your greatness. PERIOD. To step up and out authentically and unapologetically is to do so on your terms and within your control.

It was back in 2018, and I was a year away from turning forty. Like many, in honour of this milestone birthday, I had a vision of having a HUGE party. As a summer baby, I grew up always having a celebration, so there was no way this milestone was going to be an exception. And not only did I want to have a party, but I had a WHOLE vision of stepping into a trendy spot in a glittery dress, legit entering the room like Beyoncé (side note: That shit FULLY happened!). My best friend, who I lovingly refer to as "Bae," KNOWS that I am larger than life and a bit over the top. I wasn't going for a subtle celebration. Absolutely not. A girl was going for a WHOLE turn up, and so with support (and the credit card) of my loving husband, my husband and best friend put together an amazing party with all the bells and whistles: a sweet table, a candy corner, endless food, premium drinks, a photographer (who legit followed me around, capturing all of the night's events), an amazing DJ, and a photobooth. Along with the actual vision of the party, I also wanted to look a certain way. Not an uncommon desire, I went on this journey to physically transform my body. I have always been physically active and a lover of all things training, so making the shift to a more intense program to achieve the desired state I was looking for wasn't a big stretch for me.

And so began my journey. I changed my workouts, my eating and sleeping habits, upped my water intake, and just became way more diligent about my physical health. As I am sure will come as no surprise, I started to see the physical transformations—which definitely brought a smile to my face—but there was something more that I was feeling. Unable to put words to what it was, I chalked it up to a surge in energy as a result of the physical changes I was undergoing. Others around me started to also take notice, offering compliments and inquiries into what I was doing, which I happily shared. You see, I work from the ethos that if what you are doing is inspiring others to take action and make their physical, emotional, mental, social, spiritual, and sexual health a priority, then why not share your gems! Like what is the point of being great but alone? How does being on the island of "greatness" feel satisfying if you're the only one on that island, unable to share the joys with others?

You see, there remains this misnomer that women can't celebrate other women. Or that women are in constant competition with each other. Or that we don't want to see another woman do better than us. Can I just tell you how MUCH I hate that narrative? How can I as a mother, wife, co-worker, and entrepreneur speak on my achievements without showing gratitude to the women who have come before me, for those who are riding this journey with me, and for those who will come after me? There is nothing wrong with being invigorated and inspired by someone you see is doing great things, but rather than operating from a competition mindset, focus on the real outcome of collaboration, shared and cross-learning, listening and receiving. The evolution and growth of Me to Moi Health may have been my birth child, but it is being nurtured and loved on by those who want to see me grow and evolve.

Now, back to my story! As I continued on my personal journey, friends, acquaintances, and even strangers would come up to me and offer compliments, and while I was truly grateful for the love I was being shown ('cause let's be real . . . ain't no one trying to put in that work and have it not be noticeable), what I was feeling was so much more than that. You see, what was slowly becoming apparent to me is that while people were witness to my physical transformation (because I did cut weight), what I was experiencing was an emancipation of the inner chatter that prior to my journey had me questioning my power, my passion, and my purpose.

You see, for as long as I can remember, the conditions by which I was accepted, acknowledged, and promoted were based on the rules set by those around me. Hearing things like "continue to prove yourself," "work a little harder," "you're not quite there yet," and "I can see the potential" were also tied to comments such as "you may be a bit much for some," "if you tone it down a bit," and "appear a bit more agreeable" left me second-guessing myself. As someone who grew up with parents who instilled confidence and strong awareness of self, a girl was shook when she entered the workforce. While this story is not one I wish to tell, what I will quickly say is that you become very aware of the impact of your intersectionality in the education and professional environment really fast! Being a Black woman who was quite sure of herself didn't lend itself well in all environments, and so too often I was left with two options: be the outlier or "shrink" myself so others would feel more comfortable with me. Sadly, and for some time, I chose the latter. But I digress.

No one knows what we are really capable of doing until we challenge the inner chatter that too often tries to convince us that we can't, or we shouldn't, or it's not the right time, or it's not our strength—and that list goes on.

When I embarked on the physical journey, I was so hyperfocused on the physical transformation that I neglected to realize that that was not the actual win. Working out, eating and sleeping better, and drinking more water wasn't new for me, they were just something that I made adjustments to. What was new was the intention I placed in becoming the best version of myself. How many times have we embarked on a fitness journey where we achieved our desired state (loss of weight or inches) but literally felt the exact same way we did prior to the loss? Why? And again, I am going to go off on a small tangent: When it comes to weight loss, we too often do it because it is tied to a specific outcome. We have a family or school reunion, we are going on vacation, we are getting married or, like in my case, we are having a bashment, so we lose sight of everything else we gain beyond the weight. Though it took some time for me to realize, I would come to understand that this new surge in energy and focus was only mildly attributed to my new physical state, but instead fully connected to a discovery of my authentic self.

Here are a few facts about me. Those who KNOW can fully attest to them. I'm loud and opinionated, I love to wear six-inch heels and fitted clothing, I have tattoos and piercings, and I love me some trap music—you know, all the things that don't necessarily "fit" the corporate and governmental world! And while I can't particularly tell you what look they're looking for, I'm pretty sure I'm outside that circle, but as I am sure you've already figured out by now, a girl ain't bothered by not being status quo! Beyond, and perhaps more important than the things I may not be, I'm hard-working, purposeful, dependable, trustworthy, and passionate about elevating and empowering girls and women.

I'm a ride-or-die friend, I hold strong family values and connections, and I believe that everyone has agency to self-actualize. Some time ago, I had the opportunity to participate in a self-discovery session with a girlfriend of mine (who shall remain nameless because she would probably have a heart attack at the open acknowledgement of her talent, so we'll call her Michelle for story purposes) who walked me through this really powerful process that uncovered and put a name to who I was and how I operated as a human: the Anchor. Now, why do I mention this? I mention it because how many of us move through this world hiding or diminishing our gifts for fear of them not being accepted, acknowledged, or promoted?

The things we shy away from, the things we "think" make us different, are in fact the gifts and the gems that set us apart from everyone else. Perhaps people who connected with me along my physical transformation were interested in getting tips and tricks on how to implement some of the strategies in their day-to-day life, but what I finally realized is that they were actually attracted to how I was showing up in spaces—authentic and unapologetic for who I was. For so long I tried to create comfort for others around me so that they didn't think I was too loud, assertive, confident, passionate, and very self-aware, but that was my power source. That is what made me great. That is what gave me permission, power, and purpose to step into the world of entrepreneurship. Remember earlier when I talked about people "queuing you into your greatness?" I was living that because I wanted others to feel comfortable with what actually made me great. As I allowed myself to go deeper into my own personal journey, I realized that I was not only doing a disservice to myself, but I was also dishonouring the women who needed me to be their light, giving them permission to come into their own light.

You see, the weight that was lost wasn't just physical! I relinquished all the labels that had been placed on me and replaced those "labels" with words of affirmation and confirmation that finally gave me permission to live authentically. For all the certifications and degrees I had achieved, the recognition and acknowledgement of self was far more impactful than any certificate that held my name in gold writing. It wasn't the titles I held that defined who I was. Au contraire. I defined those roles by bringing my whole self to the jobs that I held. Talk about a GAME CHANGER.

It's hard to really describe what that feeling feels like, but I want to liken it to a woman's first orgasm! Whether initiated through

The greatest gift you can give to the world is giving them the best version of yourself.

self-pleasure or a partner, you know that literal mind-blowing euphoric feeling where all you can do is lie there and think to yourself, "NOW I get it!" That is the vibe I am on. You with me?

Once I became engaged in this newfound awareness, it was time to take action! For anyone who is on the cusp of coming to their big reveal, keep going. Too often after we have come to these profound realizations, we stop. We treat the "realization" as the achievement. No, no, no, no, no. That is simply the key entering the lock. It's now time to turn the key and open the door to your new place of residence where power, passion, and purpose reside.

Is it scary to step into the world of entrepreneurship? Yeah, damn right it is! Is it rewarding? Absolutely. 'Cause what do we do when it comes to doing something that we know we are destined to do? We create the narrative on why it may not be the right time, or we need to think about it more, or we need to develop a plan and all the other excuses that stop us from stepping into our purpose. The greatest gift you can give to the world is giving them the best version of yourself. And the best version of yourself can only be achieved by doing what you are called to do.

I am a student for life, so I approached this certification with the same zest and eagerness as I did with my other certifications, degrees, and Master's.

If at any point in my personal or professional life I had hit a point where I thought I was destined to be, I was mistaken, for the journey that ensued, and that I continue to be on, is in fact where life's great revelations have become truth. Can you imagine that there was a time in my life when I thought that I had pinnacle status—when I graduated with my Master's. I'm definitely not downplaying that achievement because it was a great one, but it was an achievement attached to what I thought others would regard, not what I held as the standard of achievement. Starting Me to Moi Health and affirming my gift for coaching, counselling, elevating, and empowering others to be the best version of themselves was as powerful and beautiful as the miracle of the births of my three children.

For as long as I can remember, I have found myself in positions where people sought advice and counsel. I'm not sure if it was genetically passed on to me by my parents who were both in professions of service (nursing and social work), but my passion and comfort in empowering others to recognize their capacity to take hold of their desires, wants, careers, and lives was always something that came naturally. Never chalking it up to be more than something I liked to do, I decided to take on one more certification, that of health coaching. With the sole intention of adding one more achievement to my résumé, similar to the pre-forty transformation, entry into this certification would serve as another powerful revelation that has brought me to this very privileged place of contributing to this book!

I am a student for life, so I approached this certification with the same zest and eagerness as I did with my other certifications, degrees, and Master's. I bought new binders, pens, and highlighters and was ready for all that I was going to take in over the six months of the course. Due to the intensity of the program, not only were we to learn through online courses, but we were also required to engage in "peer-to-peer" coaching (a way of practically using the techniques taught throughout the course) and have practice clients. Well, people, I am not going to lie; I wasn't overly enthused about the peer-to-peer scenario or even the practice clients, but what was to be revealed would be the birth of entrepreneurship and a heightened awareness of my personal gift.

Oblige me with a quick pivot! Have you ever found yourself receiving the same type of compliment but for doing or engaging in different things? The same type of compliments that I had received from people when I was "physically transforming" were the same types of comments I was getting from my class peers and practice clients about their experience with me. Things like "I don't know what you're doing but you are glowing." "You're on a vibe and I'm about it." "How are you so together all the time?" And my personal favourite: "I swear you're not human."

The truth is, I wasn't discovering who I wanted to be; I was becoming who I was always intended to be.

The moment I made the commitment to my personal development was the moment I relinquished all the labels and titles that were placed on me. I wasn't seeking acceptance, acknowledgement, or promotion from my colleagues or bosses. Nope. I was seeking acceptance, acknowledgement, and promotion of myself, by myself.

... I laugh and cry because it was never up to anyone but me.

Who is ANYONE to tell you where you need to grow, where you can thrive, where you have value, where you belong, and when you have been accepted? Who is anyone to tell you that now is the right time to step into the world of entrepreneurship? Mmmmmm, no one! Get all the way the *&%$ outta here! Even as I write this chapter and reflect on ALL the times I allowed someone to dictate my place in their world (not mine), I laugh and cry because it was never up to anyone but me.

For so damn long I spent my valuable time (and yes, our time is valuable) looking to hit that moment when I would "achieve" what was needed of me to be seen as worthy, when really, that is nothing we should be aiming for. If we stop at the level someone else feels we need to be at to move forward, do you realize that you may actually be undermining your fulsome capacity? I mean, has anyone really ever wanted you to be better than they are? Particularly in the workplace (and notwithstanding your parents)?

The thing is, when you step out authentically, you can't be compared to anyone else. I make that statement not because no one is better than you, but because no one IS YOU and therefore, there is no comparison. Our desire to fit a mould or achieve someone else's standard of success is based on their level of achievement, not yours. I said it before, and I will say it again: Seeking approval of achievement based on someone else's standard may be undermining your actual potential.

Now, this advice doesn't mean go out there and live rogue, not giving a %$#@ about what people think. I mean, there are still rules, and we must still live among people. What I am saying is emancipate yourself from people's desired expectation of who you should be and let them become aware of who they need to be when in your presence.

Who would've thought a very quick decision to complete my certification as a health coach would prove to be a life-altering experience? Like I'm not just a practising certified health coach, I'm the founder and owner of Me to Moi Health. If someone would have told me three years ago that I would own my own business, I would have laughed. And not because I ever doubted the things I put my mind to, but because I had finally given myself permission to be great AND to be okay with being great. I am living life and showing up authentically and unapologetically for who I am and THAT makes me unstoppable!

There is a quote by artist Christina Lonsdale that goes "being authentic will radiate more pure energy than trying to be an ideal you."

Sit with that quote for a minute. Think about all the times you tried to fit yourself into a box that you didn't fit into but that you thought was both ideal and would be accepted. How did you feel? What did you tell yourself to make it okay? I ask these questions not to fill you with guilt but to proclaim today as the last damn day you allow yourself to be ideal instead of being authentic!

YOU. Yes you. The one reading this book. The one who seeks to hide in the shadows instead of stepping into the light. The one who believes they are only here to serve instead of lead. The one who says other people's happiness is all they need for their happiness. The one who is waiting to be validated for the things they do instead of recognizing their own strength and importance. Yup, all of you. It's time to emancipate yourself from that inner chatter and begin your journey.

Writing my story was not easy. As a matter of fact, trying to collect my thoughts on the lessons learned and what I wanted to share, the words of wisdom I wanted to impart, and the imprint I wanted to leave on your mind and soul when you read this chapter did not come easy. But you see, this book isn't just about sharing our stories. This book is to remind you that your chapter awaits to be written, 'cause you are just getting started!

"Feeling gratitude and not expressing it is like wrapping a gift and not giving it."

–William Arthur Ward

First, I want to express my deepest gratitude to my parents, Daniel and Heather Saintiche, for laying roots that have not only grounded me but have been my source of strength and power. To my husband, Duane, thank you for being my co-captain and for never clipping my wings but instead creating space for me to just be me. To my children, Iman, Zariyah, and Ezekiel, who are the extension of my life's greatest achievements, thank you for being my continued source of motivation. Thank you to the greatest family and friends (who are like family) on the planet for your endless support. And to my sisterhood, thank you for pouring into my heart and soul.

Aisha Saintiche is a born and raised Montrealer who now lives in Ontario with her husband and three children. From a young age, and courtesy of her strong upbringing, Aisha always found herself in spaces where wholistic wellness was at the centre of all things personal and professional. While she holds a Master's in Public Policy, Administration and Law, her greatest academic achievement has been her certification as a health coach. Delving into a space that has always been a part of her life has become her purpose work, where she has the opportunity and privilege of empowering others to see past and emancipate themselves from the physical, mental, emotional, and spiritual barriers that keep one from achieving their desired state. As the founder and owner of Me to Moi Health, Aisha is committed to and believes that the practice of self-care is the conduit to self-awareness, self-discovery, and self-actualization. Aisha lays the foundation of her chapter through her own personal journey of self-actualization, where she steps up and out, unapologetic for who she is and ready to empower and elevate those ready to be great!

www.metomoi.com

IG @metomoi.health

“You know, ladies, we don’t spend FAR enough time shining a light on ourselves.”

Aisha Saintiche

Reflection Prompt

Write out your bio from the perspective of your BIGGEST FAN! Drop the conditions, the limiting beliefs, and the lies and BRAG about yourself. Be unapologetic in your LOVE OF SELF! Own the things that make you DIFFERENT! Step outside your space of comfort and show up in your POWER SOURCE!

Reflection Prompt

What thoughts keep you where you are? Try to write them out.

Ex: ***You can't quit. Your mom and dad paid all that money. You're lucky to even have a job . . .***

Chapter Five

"Told You So" Sincerely, Your Heart

Crystal Mank

A moment is all it takes to change your life, your world, and everything you thought you knew. For me, it was holding a child's head in my hands, my gloves covered in blood. Blood was dripping off the table so close to my new pink shoes, while an anesthesiologist tried to secure this little boy's airways as blood pooled out of his mouth and down the sides of his cheeks and onto my hands. I was suddenly alone with this boy in the sweaty, hot, overcrowded emergency room, repeating to myself, "I am a respiratory therapist, and this is my job." For me, situations like this one are nothing new. I'm used to being the one helping resuscitate patients, putting in breathing tubes, seeing the worst of the worst. It is what I signed up for. That day in the emergency room, for the first time in twelve years, I laid my armour at the door and didn't pretend like everything around me was all right; I didn't put the pressure on myself to handle this situation and tell the world that I was okay. That day changed the course of my life forever. At that moment, I decided to feel it all. I would feel this boy's life in my hands, I would feel the parents' grief, and I would let myself be human.

Growing up, I always had a deep love for people. I helped and cared for them, and I went that extra mile to make people feel good and well taken care of. I was the second of four children, and some of my fondest memories as a little girl were taking care of my baby sister and watching her grow. The only thing I ever wanted to be was a mother. My love for science and education took me to university, where I fell in love with my husband, and then off I went to college where I earned my diploma in Respiratory Therapy. I was the third in my family to become a respiratory therapist, and I had a glimpse of what my life could look like if I worked hard and put in my time. I'd have a big house, vacation multiple times a year, retire young, and provide for my growing family. I had been a people-pleaser from birth, and I could see how proud my parents and everyone around me were when I graduated and accepted a full-time job at the Hospital for Sick Children in Toronto. There were only five full-time jobs in Ontario in my graduating year, and I was one of the lucky ones. So, I headed to the big city, so excited for the adventure and what was to come. I was eager to learn and develop my skills in one of the most prestigious hospitals in the world.

Have you ever had one of those moments that just stuck with you? Kind of like those children's books where you have to choose your own adventure? Turn to page 22 if you want to continue working at

SickKids; turn to page 48 if you know this job isn't for you. That was me on my very first day. I had the perfect pencil skirt on, a nice blouse all tucked in, flats on so that I could walk faster down the halls if need be. Suddenly, alarms start ringing, pagers start beeping, and crash carts whizzed by. Over the announcements, a Code Blue was called in the Intensive Care Unit. As I stood in the back of the room observing, I witnessed my colleagues start CPR and immediately place a breathing tube into a lifeless baby. My whole body froze, tensed up, and this feeling of wanting to run out the door and never look back rushed through me. This feeling only lasted a second, yet I can remember it like yesterday now thirteen years later. At that moment, I made a choice. I turned to page 22 and chose to continue working at SickKids.

Here are all the thoughts that rushed through my head: *You can't quit; you just started; your mom and dad paid all that money for your education; you are so lucky to even have a job, unlike most of your friends from school; you are not a quitter; you get vacation time and benefits; you get to start your pension; this is how you can be of most service for people; your mom just shared in the hometown newspaper about your graduation and where you are working; you don't want to go through any more interviews; you are working at the best hospital.* So, from that moment on, I created this little room inside my head where I pushed down and hid away any more of those feelings of wanting to leave to make sure I didn't disappoint the ones I love.

I just didn't know there were any other ways to live life or choose life.

Oh, the beautiful gift of time, space, and awareness. Looking back on my first day of work and that scared little girl (me), I send her love and forgiveness and thank her for doing the best that she could at that time. I just didn't know there were any other ways to live life or choose life. I was so desperate for approval and to make people proud of me, and the only way I knew how to do that was through working hard, pushing through, and not giving up.

Over the next ten years, I got married and had four beautiful boys with my husband. And truly, from the bottom of my heart, I am so thankful for the job that allowed me to have vacation time to go on a honeymoon and have four years of paid maternity leave with my kids. These are memories I have because of the choices I made.

I know that any mother out there will say that having children changes your life. Returning to work was always met with my anxiety and stress about what I would witness or what everyday circumstances would end a child's life. My mood and energy would take a drastic 180 turn and would leave me in a whirlwind of emotions. I was in the thick of it: motherhood, being a wife, a friend, a sister, a daughter, a member of society, and anything else you want to add in there, as I'm sure I missed a few hundred things. I was exhausted, burnt out, and downright miserable. I blamed my state of being on anything and anyone I could.

Usually, when I would finally stop moving and my brain had a chance to catch up while my head hit the pillow, I would start to pray. At that point in my life, it wasn't to anyone in particular. I believe in God but didn't quite believe or have as much faith as I do today. My prayers were more out of desperation than anything else; I knew there had to be more to life. For as long as I can remember, all I ever wanted was to be a mother, but why was I desiring more now that I was a mother to four healthy, loving, beautiful boys? I was struggling to see the joy, love, and light. There had to be something more for me; I truly believed that I was made for more. I had all this frustration, anger, rage, and bitterness, which may come as a shock to those who know me since I am usually smiling on the outside. On the inside, however, I was suffocating.

It didn't take long for answers to start coming through. Well, answers that didn't seem like answers at the time. I don't think answers come with a sticky note that says, "Here is what you were asking for." It would be somewhat helpful, though, if they did! My answer first took form in a fantastic network marketing community that I am still a part of today. This community of people taught me to believe in myself and FIND the Crystal shining behind the very strategic walls I had built. I needed to get healthy from the inside out so that I could heal and stand strong in what I needed to do and share. Being a shy people-pleaser, I had a lot of work that needed to be done and still does today. First, I needed to build a belief that the voices, nudges, and feelings I was experiencing (even though no one else felt them around me) were valid, were real, and were for a damn good reason. Then, I needed to put in the grunt work of learning to love and forgive myself. I am grateful that I said yes and followed my heart.

Here is where my story comes back to the beginning, when I started to make different life choices, and when I finally started listening to my heart.

The morning of my thirty-fifth birthday, I took my dad up on his offer to treat me to breakfast, my favourite meal of the day. Over the years, my dad and I could talk about anything, or perhaps I should say that my dad loves to talk, and I usually soak in the lesson he is trying to teach me. But that day, my birthday, wasn't going to just be like any other day; my father was about to give me one of the biggest gifts he would ever give me. I can't quite remember how the conversation started; I am sure it had to do with me complaining about how exhausted I was, how much work had to be done, or something I didn't think I was doing well enough. He stopped the car, looked at me, and said, "Crystal, I know this isn't how you want to live your life. I know you don't want to be so angry all the time, and I know for sure yelling at the kids isn't who you want to be. I think you should go and meet with that woman again, you know, the one that has her soul-healing sessions. I think you need to go back to her and get her to teach you how to love yourself. I know you love everyone around you, and you give so much of yourself, but I don't think you ever really learned how to love yourself." Tears ran down my face, and I had never felt so much relief in all my life. There was no denying, no hiding from the truth. I didn't feel ashamed or embarrassed to be called out and seen without my armour on for once in my life. I knew my heart and my soul felt it too; it was time to get to work.

That day, I didn't run or hide. I ended up visiting my friend and her soul-healing circle and cried and cried and vowed from that day forward on that new day of my thirty-sixth year that I wanted to learn how to love myself. Once I set that intention into the world, a wild, beautiful ride began to get me to where I am today.

For me, it was like learning how to walk; it took time, practice, and a whole lot of grace for me to get to a place where I could look myself in the mirror and say, "I love and accept you for who you are and who you are here to be." Some of the tools that helped me were journaling feelings, thoughts, emotions, old stories, and writing out who I wanted to be. Like my soul-healing circle, joining a supportive women's group gave me a safe space to grow, share what I needed, learn from other women, and most importantly, not feel so alone. Learning how to meditate and quiet my mind helped me feel less scattered and frazzled. And please don't picture me sitting in an empty room with incense burning and soft music playing. The only time I could squeeze in this meditation was before I went to sleep, and I wasn't sure how to meditate, so I downloaded an app with guided meditations to help me get started. Meet yourself where you are and take baby steps where you can. Or maybe you can start by writing a love letter to yourself, sharing all the things you love about yourself, then read it, morning and night. Wherever you begin, honour yourself and know there is not a right or wrong way. Take your time and find joy in figuring it out, and if you need to, try again.

Once I started paying more attention to myself and my needs, things began to uproot from other areas in my life. I was becoming a different person; I was no longer that shy people-pleaser who always said yes. Instead, I started wanting newer and bigger things.

Work was getting harder and harder to leave at my job, and as I began to listen to what my heart really needed, I slowly cut back my hours at the hospital and was able to dig a little deeper into what my soul was leading me to do.

It was at a network marketing convention where I had one of my most significant breakthroughs about work. A man came on stage and asked us to write down our top goals in life: travel, business, friendship, and relationships, and when he said health goals, I started to cry. With tears streaming down my face (again, I know), I knew what I had to do. I had been working night shifts to make life easier for my family. I could make dinner, have it on the table, and then leave at 5:15 for my

7:00 p.m. start time, leaving my hubby with bedtime duties and daycare drop-off the next day. It was how we were managing and getting by. Although night shifts were helpful, needed, and better for everyone else in the family, I was suffering. I would arrive home at 9:00 a.m. and sleep until about 12:30, and then I would be up again and expecting myself to function like a normal human being, sometimes going back in for another night shift, then driving home with all the windows down in -40-degree weather just to stay awake. A running joke at work and at home was "Crystal made it home okay this time without getting into an accident or falling asleep at the wheel." So, when that man on the stage asked me to state my health goals, it was simply to be ALIVE. I would no longer be the butt of a joke of making it home okay; I was here to be more and would do something about it. With my casual position at the hospital, I made my own choice, and I decided that day I would never work another night shift again. I came home and had a very difficult conversation with my husband about not working any more nights, all the while knowing that I would add more work and pressure onto his already busy schedule.

There was so much fear behind my decision: Would my husband stay? Would he still love me even though I wouldn't be the woman he married? I was a woman finding her voice and trying to share it with the world. We had another complicated conversation at the kitchen table one night. As patient as he was in listening, I needed to get the point across that none of my actions were selfish. I knew deep down that for once, the choices and actions I was taking were the least selfish things I could ever do. Being able to voice and share those thoughts with him that night was so uncharacteristic of the past me, but it was a giant step into who I was becoming.

Slowly, I took a few more steps here and there. Then finally, I was able to start dreaming again. Who would have thought a thirty-five-year-old mother of four could have her own wishes and her own dreams and not be selfish . . . you can exhale your shock with me.

As I continued to evolve, it became necessary to carve out time for myself. I've always heard that you can't pour from an empty cup. I often felt burnt out and like I had nothing left to give. I added self-care, meditation, yoga, and taking baths to my to-do list in an attempt to fill myself back up again. But when I didn't complete those tasks or find the time to do them, I felt even more drained than when I started. What if we looked at our list of needs as necessary and non-negotiable in our daily schedule? Carving out time for myself was essential to keep me flowing. It isn't a "to-do"; it has become a part of my day, like brushing my teeth. I want good dental health as much as I want good self-love health.

I knew the day was coming. I started feeling something shifting, needing me to finally decide whether to go back to the hospital or not. It had been over a year since my last shift, and management needed a decision. My heart had given me enough time to get to where I finally needed to be. I had known for quite some time that the hospital wasn't where I was supposed to be, wasn't where I was supposed to be putting my energy . . . there was and is something more for me. My manager asked for my decision, return to work or resign. Even though I knew it was coming, the gravity of the decision still shot right through me, right to my core.

So, how do you leave? How do you tell your husband that you don't want to go back? How do you tell your manager, your colleagues, and the ones in the trenches with you that you have found the golden ticket out of there and you're leaving them all behind? How do you justify wanting to leave a good job to start over, to start from scratch, from nothing? How do you justify not bringing in any income during a worldwide pandemic that is causing people to lose their jobs, and you have a stable one? How do you look your lover in the eyes and say, "I know I am not the same person you married, but I know what I have to do." How do you trust that they will still love you, support you, and stand by you through it all? How do you take that leap of faith? How do you jump without a parachute?

What if we looked at our list of needs as necessary and non-negotiable in our daily schedule?

Wouldn't it just be easier if you could see the end of the movie before you had to make that leap? Easier to know that it will be a soft landing when you jump? With what I am learning and feeling, this leap is what faith is all about. I was taught about it in Sunday School and have read all about trusting and letting go and believing you are right where you need to be. But when it is your turn to really trust and let go, that is where true faith is found.

So, once again, my husband and I sat down at the kitchen table to figure it out. I confessed that my heart couldn't go back. I couldn't be the one to disconnect a child from a ventilator one more time. I couldn't be the one to catch a mother as she fell to the floor one more time. Through my tears and heart-shaking fear, I told my husband I wouldn't be going back. He got quiet, which is how he processes, and I'm sure I might have a few superpowers, or because we have been married so long, but I knew exactly what he was thinking without him even saying anything. I looked at him through my tear-filled eyes and said, "You think I am being dramatic, don't you?" Quietly, he said, "Yes, that is exactly what I am thinking." It was tough to hear, but I allowed him to state his feelings, then left the room feeling gutted.

I know he loves me, I know he knew how hard my days at work could be, and I know he only wants the best for our family and me. I know his fear of not having enough and not providing or keeping our lifestyle was what was playing out in his mind. How could we manage to run our house on his paycheque alone? I 100 percent got it and am so thankful for all he does. But at that moment, as I walked away, I knew that I could no longer stay in a job that left me empty, that was distracting me and keeping me away from where I was supposed to be. I finally saw strength in knowing that my choice was exactly where I needed to be and what I was supposed to do. I am fully supported in my faith in every sense: financial, emotional, spiritual, mental, and physical, in every possible way. If I leap, if I choose ME, choose my heart, I will never not have enough. I knew at that moment that saying goodbye to everything I had built over the last thirteen years was the start of something new. Was it hard to write that resignation letter? HELL YES! Was it even harder to tell my husband I wasn't going back? Was it hard knowing that he could decide to not love me anymore for making such a massive decision without him? HELL YES! Was I prepared to go one more day without following my truth? NO!

Within two months of leaving SickKids, we began building our dream. I have dreamt this dream so many times and in so many different ways. We have fully renovated our old animal barn into a beautiful venue space. We host weddings, family reunions, women's retreats, holiday markets, photoshoots, corporate events, etc. I mean, I could go on and on, but really, the possibilities are endless. Just as I had been searching all those years ago, I wanted to find a space to care for people, help people feel taken care of and, most importantly, feel loved. Bit by bit, piece by piece, I keep seeing our dreams come true. We hosted our very first wedding not long ago, and we are hosting our first women's retreat this fall. To say that my heart is full is an understatement.

Never give up on those whispers from your heart, even when no one else understands them or backs you up. Trust that you have unlimited resources at your fingertips, and even though it's hard, you are being led right to where you are meant to be.

This chapter is dedicated to my mother, Catherine. Without you, none of this would be possible. Thank you for always believing in me and helping me shine.

To all the people I have worked with over the years, near and far, you have a special place in my heart. Your endless love and sacrifice for others don't go unnoticed a single day in my eyes. I know your experience doesn't have to be mine, just as I know I don't need to justify mine in any way. These stories are not meant to make you feel weak or unimportant for not making the leap like I did. This was my story and my timing, and for me to live my truth, I knew it was time to leave. From the bottom of my heart, I pray that if you need help or feel lost, hopeless, or tired, please reach out to someone and talk. Take time off, even if you can't afford it, because it is you who is left at the end of the day.

Thank you for being here and allowing me to share my heart with all of you.

Crystal Mank has a light about her that in the moment you meet her, you know she is someone special. She is someone who will go above and beyond for you, who will listen without judgment, and who will hold space for you to grow and heal. Crystal is a mother to four active and loud boys and is beginning to find herself outside of them. She is a loving wife to her husband, Jeremy, and can't wait to build their dream wedding and retreat venue together on their beautiful seventy-eight-acre estate. Crystal resigned from Toronto's Hospital for Sick Children in May 2021 where she was a respiratory therapist for the past thirteen years, working in the Pediatric and Neonatal Intensive Care Unit as well as the emergency department and clinical wards. Crystal is excited to start this new chapter, even through the bumps and challenges of love, relationships, and work. She is learning to let go and forgive. This world is a beautiful place full of opportunity and growth, and it is waiting for Crystal to open herself up to endless possibilities.

www.ontheridgeevents.com

"I finally saw strength in knowing that my choice was exactly where I needed to be and what I was supposed to do. I am fully supported in my faith in every sense: financial, emotional, spiritual, mental, and physical, in every possible way. If I leap, if I choose ME, choose my heart, I will never not have enough."

Crystal Mank

Reflection Prompt

Besides the limiting beliefs you carry, what are the actual things/people/jobs in your life that are keeping you distracted and away from where you are meant to be?

Reflection Prompt

What's holding you back today from taking the leap into YOUR dreams?

Is it the fear of people not liking you? Not validating you? Accepting you? Wanting you?

Dig deep!

Chapter Six

Keep It Simple

Kelly Jane Thorne

Have you ever felt like you were at a crossroads in life, knowing a decision needed to be made that could change the trajectory of your life forever?

Being at a crossroads can feel scary; just one tiny decision can make your life look completely different. Okay, maybe it's a big decision, but nonetheless, you have a decision to make.

All you know is that you don't like the direction you're headed, and you HAVE TO change course. One of the hardest parts of being stuck at a crossroad is how isolating and terrifying it can be. It can feel like no one totally understands, and you alone have to decide which direction to take.

That's a great deal of pressure for one person, especially when you've spent a lifetime abandoning yourself, believing you made the wrong decisions, and losing sight of your intuition. You are paralyzed by the options and have no idea which direction to take, while knowing deep down that your life depends on the next "right" choice. This choice matters. This choice will set the course for everything that happens next.

On July 7, 2017, I found myself "graduating" from a treatment centre in downtown Toronto. I spent six weeks of my life healing from a disease I didn't think I had. Denial, just like alcoholism, is powerful. It prevents us from seeing reality and accepting consequences. I knew my life was a mess, but it certainly wasn't my fault.

I was a queen of deflecting and placing blame on everyone but myself. If I'm not at fault, then I don't have to do the hard work of looking at myself. The damage, however, is that you will never be able to create the change you desire.

It all starts with me.

I had to accept responsibility. I had to take ownership, or nothing was ever going to change.

So, on July 7, I walked out of that treatment centre with a new lease on life. It's amazing what you can learn about yourself in a few short weeks when you've been plucked from the life you knew and are forced to figure out who you truly are, all without the presence of substances or alcohol.

I was there to do the work, and I was ready to heal. Upon leaving the treatment centre, I had two choices: I could continue on the path I had been on, or I could forge a new path and see where that new road could lead. I knew where the past path had brought me, and I didn't want to go back there.

I had been living on autopilot for years, going through the motions and continually asking, "Is this all there is? Is this what my life has come to?" I had become numb to the chaos and choices in my home, and after thirteen years of addiction and a rocky marriage, I left, taking the last bit of courage with me.

Addiction raged like wildfire in our home, and I knew if I was going to get out alive, I had to save myself. Everything we had worked toward was gone. My identity was tied to being the perfect wife, with the gorgeous home, and the most beautifully perfect kids—essentially, everything but the white picket fence. We had the "million-dollar family" and were envied by many. We were the million-dollar family that was drowning in a sea of debt. The addiction changed us. I became a version of myself that I no longer recognized. Scraping myself off the ground, I slowly inched my way forward.

As a mom just barely hanging on, I put unrealistic expectations on myself to create a better life for my kids than the one they had before, a life free from conflict, pain, and discomfort. I know now that this life is not possible, as I am not God. I wanted them to know that despite losing it all, opportunities and abundance were everywhere, even if I didn't entirely believe it myself.

The first decision I made was to move to my mother's house. With two young children beside me, I felt this choice was the safest way I knew to get back on my feet. We would be supported and protected there. I know not everyone has this luxury, and I recognize how very fortunate I am and thank God daily for this gift. Part of my legacy includes creating a safe space for women to go, a place where they can leave an abusive relationship and get the clarity they need before taking the next steps.

As I sought to get back on my feet, I knew my kids were watching me. They were counting on me; thus, messing up was not an option. In order to be present for my children, I had to make decisions with a clarity not yet experienced. It was essential that I got clean and sober. I was ready to look in the mirror and confront my addiction to alcohol. For the first time in my life, I began to question the person staring back in the glass. ***Who are you? What do YOU really want? Why are you here? What is your purpose in life? Was all this pain meant for something larger than you?*** I didn't know it then, but those questions would follow me in the years to come.

Sunday, April 15, 2017

I surrendered and said goodbye to alcohol. Shortly after, I decided to go to treatment. I was determined to tackle my addiction for good. There are multiple layers to addiction, and I was going to uncover them one by one. I had stuffed my feelings, thoughts, and experiences down for so long that I couldn't carry the load anymore. I needed to share. I needed to speak my truth. I needed to let people in if I was going to get the help I desired. It was at the treatment centre, with the help and support of my counsellors that I found the strength and courage to advocate for my needs and stand firm in my decision to leave my marriage forever, something I had tried to do unsuccessfully on my own for years. A history of codependency and addictive relationships proved it was vital that I get support in this area. A third party would facilitate the conversation for me and would assure that I spoke my truth.

The road to recovery is long and winding. I focused on my physical addiction first, as being present was a top priority. If I wasn't clean and sober, I wouldn't be able to provide stability for my family.

Getting there was scary; I continually came face-to-face with the person staring back in the mirror. For many years, looking in the mirror was painful, and it tore me apart. It hurt. I was so full of regret, shame, guilt, and disgust. I didn't like who I had become. I didn't know who she was anymore. Addiction changed who I was and brought me to depths I never thought I'd go. I did things that I am not proud of, and I allowed things to be done to me that make me cringe to think about to this day. Looking in the mirror was excruciating. I forced myself daily to look into my eyes, each day searching for the little girl that was me:

the one with the bright smile and bright blonde hair. I was sunshine, as they called me, and the light in my parents' eyes.

Where was she? Where did she go? Where was the little girl I had abandoned all those years ago?

I had to find her.

I had to reconnect with her. I had to reconnect to myself.

My journey of self-discovery began with learning to love myself. With the guidance of counsellors, therapy, and my sponsor, I began to peel back the layers. I dove headfirst into the 12-step program. I became honest with myself and with others. We can't genuinely heal if we are still hiding pieces of our truth. I decided if people were going to get to know me, they were going to get to know the real me, not the made-up version of myself that I put out on display. They were gonna get the real deal, with all my quirks, scars, and flaws. What I discovered was that the more authentic I became, the more my true personality began to shine through.

It hasn't been easy. Sometimes, we have to go through hell so we can find our heaven. There have been twists and turns, highs and lows, and each time I felt like I was losing my grip, I'd regroup and keep pushing forward. Going backward was not an option.

I started paying attention to what was happening in the world around me. My life had been so small before; I didn't even have my own social media account. I was isolated from everyone.

What I discovered was that the more authentic I became, the more my true personality began to shine through.

In the early months of my recovery, a woman came into my world via social media where she shared her story of her family's experience with addiction. I felt like she saw right through me. For the first time, I didn't feel so alone. There was someone else out there who had experienced my pain. There was someone else out there who felt as alone and isolated as I was, and yet here she was. Showing up. Showing up publicly and sharing her story. She wasn't broadcasting the gory details, she wasn't doing it for attention, she was doing it so that she could help one woman, one person. And that person was me. I became a silent follower for months and eventually found the courage to reach out and send her a private message. I knew without a shadow of a doubt that this woman was sent to light the way for me. To show me what is possible. To show me that my story matters. My story does not define me. She told me that my story would one day be my gift, a sacred gift that I could share with the world. I didn't believe it then, but I do now. I know with conviction that my story was meant for a greater purpose. It is my aspiration that every woman walking in my shoes feels the support, love, and hope that I did.

My journey into entrepreneurship started slowly. I wasn't even sure I had something to share or create. I just knew I had a story. Shortly after meeting this incredible woman, Marsha Vanwynsberghe, at a live event, we began to work together, and she became my very first coach. I was new to the world of coaching and had no idea how it worked. I felt like I was ready for the next step of my journey. Marsha became the mentor and guide that I needed. She taught me how to take ownership of my story and to share the lessons. When we met, I was in survival mode; there were still a lot of personal life challenges and fires to put out.

"When the student is ready, the teacher appears." –Buddhist quote

One of my greatest assets was my ability to keep an open mind. I was open to receiving and doing, even if I didn't immediately understand why. I trusted. My way wasn't working and hadn't been for a long time. Through our weekly coaching sessions, I eventually got to a space where I was beginning to thrive, not just survive.

One-on-one coaching led to group coaching programs, specifically designed to build a business from my story, which opened up my world to more women, just like me, who had powerful stories to share. These women supported me and loved me just as I was. They provided a safe space for me to grow and encouraged me to show up and challenge myself in ways I never thought possible. It was through our vulnerability that we began to see that we are more alike than we are different. There was no competition, only a deeper desire and understanding that we were chosen to do more. We had gifts to share with the world.

I was asked to speak at events. My story, my gift, my lessons—they were no longer for me. I had to get out of my own way. What if my story was the solution someone was looking for? What if my story changed someone's life? What if my story offered hope?

I spoke at the school where I worked, the very place I feared showing up as my true self. This time was different. This time I was growing into the woman I wanted to be. I was confident in who I was becoming and the lessons I had to share. I wanted to be the solution, which meant serving a greater purpose. A student came to me months later and told me he had stopped using drugs because of my story. That is the power of impact. His story became my fuel to show up even more. Without hesitation. Without fear.

One life.

It all started with me wanting to save one life. Now, I want to save every woman or child who has walked in my path. I want to bring awareness to families who are living with addiction. I want to help women affected by addiction find freedom in their own lives. My big vision is big. My vision is to provide a treatment centre just for women and children, a sanctuary where women can come to unpack and heal their stories. It will be a safe place for them to rediscover themselves, as I once did.

I speak on addiction, the gifts of recovery, codependency, using your voice, trusting your intuition, co-parenting through addiction, communication, boundaries, and courage.

Using my voice is new for me. As a young girl, I kept thoughts and opinions to myself, afraid of being rejected by others. I stayed quiet, even when it hurt me. I didn't use my voice. It wasn't until I had a child of my own that I realized I had to be the one to break those patterns. It was on me to shift, and one of the ways I shifted was by becoming an author in the collaborative book *Owning Your Choices* led by Marsha Vanwynsberghe. Being an author has been a dream of mine from a very young age, and I wanted my children to see what was possible. It always felt so far out of reach, and here it was, presented right to me. I had to write! I loved to write! Writing, for me, was how I processed my emotions and how I made sense of my stories. Writing, for me, was another tool on my healing journey.

I put an extreme amount of pressure on myself as a single parent, something I remind myself daily NOT to do. Not only did I put the burden on myself to rebuild our lives financially, but I also had to rebuild our lives emotionally and spiritually. I do my best to give myself a lot of space, grace, and compassion about it.

Trying to figure out what I wanted to do next wasn't easy, even with amazing coaches. I often felt like I was chasing the next shiny thing. To be completely honest, I feel lost again today. It's okay, though; the unknown is where the magic lies. It's not so scary anymore.

Building a business is hard. I've wanted to quit more times than I care to admit, and not because I don't love what I'm doing, because I do.

Building a business is hard. I've wanted to quit more times than I care to admit, and not because I don't love what I'm doing, because I do. I want transformation and growth for everyone. I want to make an impact on people's lives. I want that more than anything.

It's just that shit got hard. Building a business is a whole new level of healing and personal growth. It requires work, a work ethic, consistency, resilience, and unwavering belief. It also requires letting go and not being attached to the outcome. Doing it for praise, approval, or accolades will always leave you feeling empty. I had to release all expectations of how it was going to land or who was going to receive it. I had no control over that. Showing up, using my voice, sharing my story, going live . . . at times it was frickin' hard. It still is sometimes, but I've just gotten used to the discomfort, and with practice, it does get easier. It gets easier because each day I trust myself a little bit more.

As someone who put unrealistic expectations on myself and attached my self-worth to my financial success, it made it even more difficult to continue when I didn't see the monetary gains and rewards up front. It also became apparent that I had a self-worth/money story to work through too. My self-worth is not dependent on my net worth. I used to thrive off immediate gratification; I wanted the quick fix, and when it didn't come, I got discouraged. I thought my success was going to happen overnight, and when it didn't go my way, I felt like maybe I just wasn't cut out for it. Perhaps I wasn't good enough, or maybe I was asking too much? Shouldn't I be content with where I was, and what I had then? Right? I mean, I had a great job, and I was changing lives at school. Shouldn't that be enough? I guess if it were, I wouldn't feel the yearning and burning desire to do more. So, after a few failed launches and some tweaking of programs, I was back at it again. Again, I had to put my ego aside. It wasn't about me, it's about all the women I support.

Creating a business is a long game. Everyone told me this fact, but I didn't believe them.

In the spring of 2020, the COVID-19 pandemic gave me the space I had been praying for. It gave me a break in my schedule to create something and focus on building my business. Being a single parent, working full time, and having kids in travel sports proved challenging as I tried to incorporate new business interests into my day. So, while our country headed into the first of many lockdowns to come, I headed for my laptop and began forming a virtual community.

I wanted to create something that would bring families together during a time that was beginning to isolate us all.

Unstoppable Families emerged. The purpose of this group was to bring families, fitness, and fun to the forefront. It had nothing to do with my desire to serve women living alongside addiction, which got put on the back burner for a bit as the country grappled to find new ways to cope. I introduced weekly mindset themes, activities, and challenges. I lined up guest speakers to provide value and support. I learned Canva like nobody's business, and I created a space where I could show up daily and support people along the way.

People took notice. I took notice. I began to see what I was capable of. I began to lean into my gifts and talents, something I had suppressed for so long.

Fear of showing up had kept me stuck.

I was done.

I was done giving into fear.

I was done letting my inner critic win.

I was done trying to be "perfect."

I took action. Messy action.

Through it all, I proved to myself that I could do anything I put my mind to as long as it was in alignment with my purpose. I was offered leadership positions that introduced me to a whole new level of growth. I began to see and feel what it meant to be in complete alignment. I started a Facebook group for women who were living alongside addiction. I poured into them and served them so they knew they were not alone. This group continues to evolve, and I've now opened up the space for all women, not just the ones living with addiction. Boundaries, codependency, trusting our intuition, using our voice . . . these are universal truths that apply to us all.

As I look back on my time with Unstoppable Families, after ten weeks of delivering content, I began to burn out. It was a lot for me. I felt the pressure to show up every day, all day, and I noticed that my sole purpose for doing so was to bring families together, yet I was getting further and further away from my own. If creating a better life for my kids meant that I would be seeing them less, then I have failed in doing the very thing I set out to do. My kids were being worked into my schedule, and they were getting the slivers of time I had left, something I had not envisioned at all. My addictive personality was in overdrive, and I felt like I was missing out on the two people who were right in front of me, my reason for everything: my children, Michael and Ava. They are always watching. I want to be an example and set the bar higher so they can see what is possible if they believe, but none of that matters if I am so busy in the online communities that I fail to connect with the people in front of me. Whether it's drugs, alcohol, social media, or work, all these things can keep us disconnected from the people we want to connect with the most.

Overcoming alcohol addiction was just one piece of the puzzle. My feelings of not being enough, not doing enough, and not having enough are ever present. They can run me into the ground if I don't remind myself to stay in gratitude for what I have and how far I've come.

Addiction and unmanageability present themselves in many forms. The overwhelm creeps up on me if I'm not vigilant in keeping balance and boundaries and in protecting my time. I no longer say yes to everything that comes my way. I don't overbook myself because I know that it runs me down. I crave my alone time. Giving myself this space recharges me in a way that nothing else can. I check my calendar daily, I am intentional with my time, and I no longer fly by the seat of my pants. My morning routine consists of exercise, being outside, reading, and/or journaling. I don't force things. If I need to sleep in (and have the opportunity to), I do. I don't engage with people or conversations that don't light me up. I disassociate with people who are toxic to me. I can love them from afar, but they don't take up space or energy in my heart like they used to.

I have many ideas, and I want to do all of them. I've also come to realize that I don't have to do them all at once. Neither do you.

You can trust the journey, even if your path is unclear.

I fell into the trap of hiring more coaches and taking more programs. I was chasing the next best thing. I wanted them to do the work for me. I thought they had the magic elixir that was going to catapult me to the next level. I already had everything I needed, I just had to start. There is no finish line; we are always growing and always changing. You can trust the journey, even if your path is unclear. All the ups, downs, pivots, and falls. It is always about the journey. We have no control over how it goes. We can either bring fun and ease into our day, or we can force and manipulate the outcome. You get to choose.

As I reflect on my experience with addiction, I did not lose everything as I once thought. It did not break me. Instead, it taught me how to rebuild. It taught me how to create a life that I can be proud of. What I gained through the devastation was so much more than I could have imagined.

I found myself. I like myself. Heck, I actually love myself. I use my voice and advocate for my needs. I teach others to do the same. I discovered who I was at my core and am amazed at the woman staring back at me in the glass. Through my sobriety, I was able to create new friendships with deeper connections. Through my story, I have met women who have become my best friends. We see and understand each other in a way that no one else can. I asked for help, and I got so much more in return.

I have sisters all across this great earth, women who are moving mountains and learning to rise, often daily! These women are warriors, and ***we are just getting started.***

There are women praying for the answers I have; women who need to hear my story. Perhaps it's even you. I want you to know that you are not alone. I want you to experience the kind of freedom that I have discovered, the kind that makes you feel light on your feet.

I get messages all the time from women telling me they left an unhealthy marriage or relationship. I secretly, and sometimes not so secretly, jump for joy. This news sets my soul on fire. A woman's worth, whether personal or business, should not be connected to someone liking us, validating us, accepting us, or wanting us. Our freedom lies in discovering who we are and in choosing ourselves EVERY. SINGLE. DAY.

Choosing yourself is the most honourable, self-respecting, and loving thing that you can do. I want our daughters to see that they can choose themselves too.

I want women leading the way for future generations, and I want our sons and daughters to know that when we rise, we can all rise together.

Using our voice, speaking our truth, and stepping boldly into our purpose—it doesn't get much better than that.

If you are still trying to find your purpose, hang tight. You won't have to look far, as your purpose will find you when the time is right.

Listen closely to the whispers and lean into your heart. It always knows the way.

This book is dedicated to my journey.

For without this journey, the pain, the heartache, the struggle, I would not be where I am today. I am grateful for the lessons, as they all brought me to this very place and back home to myself.

To my children, Michael and Ava, the ones who are always watching. You are the greatest gift any mother could hope for. It is because of you and for you that I have grown into the mom I am today. You have taught me resilience, courage, vulnerability, trust, and love. Thank you for your unwavering support through all my ideas and dreams for the future.

Mom and Dad, it is because of you that this fire continues to burn inside of me, the fire that even during my darkest days never died. You taught me how to persevere through adversity with love and grace. There is not a day that goes by that I am not reminded of how blessed I have been to have a safe place to land and spread my wings. You believed in me when no one else did, and while you may not have always understood the path, you were always by my side.

To my brother, Mike, the first entrepreneur of the family. You inspire me daily.

To my gramma, who is 102 as I write this chapter. This book, my stories, are for you. They are for you and all the warrior women who came before you and paved the way so that I may use my voice today.

To my stepfather, Jim, although you cannot read this chapter in person, I know you are looking down with love. Thank you for guiding me and loving me and my children as your own.

To all the ones who believed I could, even when I had no belief in myself. Thank you.

Thank you for always knowing I would find a way and encouraging me every step of my journey.

Finally, to all the women who have had an impact on my journey. You have taught me how to show up, speak my truth, lead myself, and stand on the shoulders of my story. It is through your guidance, leadership, and coaching that I have seen what is possible.

Kelly Jane Thorne is a Canadian speaker, coach, teacher, and author. She is a single mom to twins and will always be an advocate for families living alongside addiction. Her mission is to help families affected by addiction find freedom in their own lives, remove guilt, and empower themselves on their own journey of self-discovery. Through her own story of recovery, Kelly has had to learn how to navigate co-parenting, communicate effectively, and implement consistent boundaries in her life and relationships. When Kelly shifted her story from blame to ownership, she began to create the change she was so desperately searching for. Kelly offers coaching and programs dedicated to helping women trust and use their voice, build their courage, and create freedom in their own lives.

"A woman's worth, whether personal or business, should not be connected to someone liking us, validating us, accepting us, or wanting us. Our freedom lies in discovering who we are and choosing ourselves EVERY. SINGLE. DAY."

Kelly Jane Thorne

Reflection Prompt

How can you begin to release the need to feel liked, validated, accepted, and wanted by others?
What will you do TODAY to choose yourself?
What about tomorrow?

Reflection Prompt

Where have you shown up with "hustle" mentality in your life? When and where have you prioritized busyness?

What insecurity was this busyness filling for you?

Chapter Seven

From Burnout and Stress to Ease + Success

Vanessa West

Growing up, I often felt lost. I had no clue what I wanted to do with my life and quickly started to realize that academics were not my strong suit. Although I would later become a work-obsessed overachiever, in high school and university, I struggled to keep up, did the bare minimum, and did not take my classes or future seriously.

From an early age I was taught that studying hard, achieving good grades, and getting into post-secondary school was the only path to achieving a high level of success. Most of my family was well educated and career driven. All my friends were achieving honour-roll grades and getting into their first-choice universities, yet I found myself struggling to find the motivation to fully apply myself.

I can remember handing in assignments late and laughing about my less-than-perfect grades. At one point, I drove to my teacher's house after school to drop off my extremely late assignment in her mailbox. I specifically remember the look of shock and disbelief on her face. My friends and I still laugh about it to this day, especially when considering how completely obsessed with timelines and organization I am now.

Throughout my teenage years and into my early twenties, I always felt that I was steps behind everyone else and was never going to catch up. I was the one in my circle of friends who was constantly trying to figure out her shit while the others seemed to have already found their paths.

After graduating high school, I headed to college to pursue aesthetics and dropped out after one week. After visiting my friends at university, I felt that I was missing out on the university experience and wanted to give it a try. Unfortunately, my grades were slacking, so I decided to repeat grade 12 and headed to university the following year.

After completing two years at the University of Guelph, I struggled to find interest in my classes and once again found myself doing the bare minimum to pass. At the time, I was very hard on myself and could not understand why I had no motivation to do better. However, this pattern continued and barely passing turned into failing. Once again, I decided to take a break from university rather than waste more money on tuition fees that were clearly getting me nowhere.

After dropping out of university, I felt more lost than ever. I had to move back home to regroup. I worked a few different jobs and moved around to try and find myself, but at this point, my self-esteem was lower than ever. I still had no idea what I wanted to do with my life.

Fortunately, I always had the option to work for my dad's painting business back home. He loved having me around, but whenever I ended up back there, I couldn't help but feel like a complete failure. To me, being back home meant that my attempt to find my career still wasn't working out.

With a little extra time on my hands, I decided to plan a New Year's Eve party in my hometown. My friends and I were sick of ending up at someone's shitty garage party or going to the city and paying for overpriced drinks and expensive hotels.

Originally, it was just going to be a small gathering, but I decided to open it to the public and rented an event space. Everyone was always scrambling to find NYE plans, so I thought, why not give it a try?! I loved planning social gatherings for my friends. I was usually the one coordinating the hangouts or group activities, so planning this party came naturally to me. I organized the bar, the DJ, the décor, and the food—I wanted it to be a good party!

My family (and some friends) thought I was completely nuts and were very worried about the liabilities associated with throwing a party of this magnitude, especially since I had no experience. To cover my ass, I hired a professional security team, purchased event insurance, and booked a school bus to drive everyone home to ensure there was no drinking and driving. Everyone was still trying to convince me that the party was a major risk, but once I had the idea in my head, no one could stop me. Weeks in advance, I sold out at a hundred tickets, with a significant wait-list due to venue capacity.

The event was a huge success with great reviews, and we only ended up with one broken window that fortunately, I was able to easily cover with my earnings.

That night I discovered a part of myself I never knew I had within me. It was the start of my career in event planning and entrepreneurship. I remember looking around and seeing everyone having a great time with huge smiles on their faces and thinking to myself, *Holy shit! I did this. Me! The girl who was always so disorganized and had just dropped out of school for the second time. I'm not a failure. I'm not lazy. I just hadn't yet found what inspired me!*

On New Year's Day, I found myself online, signing up for event-management courses. A fire was lit in me that I never had before. I became obsessed with organization and slowly figured out how to better manage my time. That year I found the confidence to finish my university degree virtually so that I could apply to the Humber Public Relations postgraduate program. This program offered a combined focus on events and marketing, so I felt it would open a lot of doors for me. I was finally starting to feel a sense of accomplishment and direction.

Before I headed to Humber, I also completed my certification in wedding planning. This side of the event industry became very appealing to me after helping out with a family member's wedding day. A large part of this course focused on how to start up and successfully run your own wedding-planning business. I was all in!

I decided on Vanessa West Events for my business name, I had a close friend design my logo, and I began to learn about web design and branding photography. I started organizing my own "styled shoots" to create usable content for my website and social media. I instantly loved this part of my business!

I remember feeling excited and overwhelmed at the same time. I learned MANY things the hard way. Business coaching or "community over competition" was not as popular at the time, so I often felt very alone on this journey of entrepreneurship.

When I first launched, it was very difficult to find clients. Around that time, it seemed wedding planning or "day-of coordination" was perceived as luxury or unnecessary. My first client was a family member I had contacted so that I could gain experience. I remember reaching out to many newly engaged couples in our hometown and asking if I could coordinate their wedding day to build my portfolio, which resulted in me putting myself in a lot of stressful situations for little to no pay. As someone who now heavily values their time and energy, I totally cringe at the thought of that memory!

I began to invest more time and money into my website and branding photography in order to look more professional and to be taken seriously. I started coordinating weddings for friends and family, and I slowly grew from there. Soon after launching my new website, I started to receive inquiries from outside my circle, and I booked my first paid-in-full client. They didn't even ask for a discount!

At this point, my long-term goal was to work at an agency in downtown Toronto, so I played it safe and kept growing my business on the side while I finished my postgraduate degree at Humber.

Even with my degree, postgraduate certificate, and co-op experience, I quickly learned how competitive the job market is in Toronto. I must have applied for 200+ jobs. I felt so defeated. I was living with my boyfriend (now husband) in Toronto and could barely cover my side of the rent with my dwindling savings. At the time, my business didn't make enough to cover my expenses, so I made the difficult decision to go work with my dad back home during the week so I could earn some money while I searched for a full-time job in the city. My now husband was so supportive through this whole process and often covered the rent when I couldn't make ends meet.

Email after email, I was notified that I didn't get the job. I remember painting a client's house while working for my dad and seeing an email on my phone from the latest company I had interviewed with shortly before. The email title seemed positive, so I was hopeful that it was finally an offer! To my disappointment, I opened it up to see the classic line "regret to inform you." I was so mentally exhausted at this point that tears instantly started streaming down my face, all while I was up on a ladder painting crown moulding. I can remember that moment so vividly because for the first time in years, I felt like a failure again.

I had done everything they told us to do in high school. I got my university degree, a postgraduate degree, event certificates, co-op experience, and volunteer work—it still wasn't enough.

I was so desperate to be back in Toronto with my boyfriend that I took on three part-time jobs that were all event related while managing my event-planning business. After a year of this endless routine, and while continuing to apply for other jobs, I was finally offered a permanent position at a marketing agency in downtown Toronto. It felt like a major win.

My event-planning business started to book up in the summers; however, my long-term goal at the time was to work my way up the corporate ladder. I didn't believe that I was even capable of scaling my event-planning business to support myself full time. I would look up to big wedding planners in Toronto and think, *That could never be me.* I put minimal effort into marketing and was okay with Vanessa West Events just being a side hustle to keep my entrepreneurial spirit alive.

Landing my first permanent job gave me a sense of security and purpose that I never had had before. For the first time ever, I finally felt like I had my shit together. I kept pushing myself to work harder and to show how committed I was to my role. The more I pushed myself, the more praise I received from my managers and family members.

I became obsessed with my new corporate job and quickly fell into the toxic agency culture. I often would brag about how many hours I worked to friends or family. I now cringe at the thought of me happily saying I was working 100+ hour weeks between my day job and my side hustle, and on minimal sleep, and laugh about it. I had no idea the damage I was doing to my body by being in a constant state of high stress; I only wanted to keep pushing. This toxic agency culture taught me a lot of work habits that I would bring into my side hustle. I continued to take on more and more and would work weddings every weekend throughout the summer in addition to working full time throughout the week.

In addition to my wedding-planning business, I co-founded a wedding directory, blog, and online shop with my cousin. We created an online platform for couples to find trustworthy vendors to plan their dream wedding. They could also find inspiration from featured local weddings and shop for cards, bridal swag, wedding planners, and bridal gift boxes, etc. It was a lot of fun but soon became an overwhelming task.

Around this time, I also started practising photography and began shooting as a wedding photographer's assistant. I tried out a few other styles of photography and soon realized my favourite was branding and boudoir—so why not start *another* business?! Everyone always said to me, "I don't know how you do it," and for a while I was able to maintain it all, until everything collectively started to get busier and busier.

I soon started to base my self-worth on my job title, busyness, and income. I continued to work long hours and did not prioritize my health. It was my work above all else. I continued to juggle my full-time job with my own side businesses.

I often went to sleep just wishing the morning would come so I could get back to work. If I were to visit my friends, I would count down the minutes until I could get back to my computer screen and my to-do list. If I started working after 10:00 a.m. on a Saturday or Sunday, I would be livid with myself, thinking how I had wasted "productive" hours. Each day I calculated how many hours I had left in the day to be as productive as possible.

As you read these words, you can probably tell I was on a fast path to burnout. I had never experienced the feeling of "burnout" before, and it hit me like a ton of bricks. I started to dislike my job. I was mentally exhausted and angry for letting myself fall so far into these toxic work habits. By this time, my wedding businesses were established, but I didn't have the energy to take anything on. My passion was gone, and I was running on fumes. I started to turn away work, and I did not want anything to do with the wedding industry. I must have turned down twenty-plus weddings that year.

I thought I was invincible and could work endless hours without any consequences, while putting in no effort to take care of myself. Looking back, I should have left my corporate job. But at the time, I still didn't fully understand my true worth as a person or value my health, so I

It took a long time before I started to invest in my health instead of just investing in my businesses and career growth.

stayed, and the cycle continued.

I felt like I was constantly chasing this "high" of approval after spending so many years feeling like a failure. As someone who was also used to being in a constant state of "struggle," I started to experience anxiety about positive things actually working out for me. Instead of addressing this issue head on, I continued to overwork and overcommit myself so there would be no mental capacity or time for me to feel anxious. I was always worried about something bad happening, even though I had a stable job, a supportive husband, and growing side hustles. I felt as if there was a limit to my success and my happiness because I was so used to being in a constant state of stress.

"Anxiety" was not even a part of my vocabulary before reaching this point of burnout. I felt like I was in a constant battle of knowing that I needed to take care of myself and feeling like I wasn't accomplishing enough. I would take vacation days and work the entire time. On one of the vacations where I had no access to the internet, I had a full-on breakdown and needed to get back home to my email inbox. I was incapable of relaxing unless it was a scheduled spa day. Even then, I would think about my to-do list.

My manager worked with me to find some work–life balance, but I started to realize that anytime I had a manageable workload at my day job, I would subconsciously fill up my schedule with my own business "to-do" list so I didn't have to deal with my anxiety. I recognized I had become this work-obsessed shell of a person, but I still wasn't at a point where I wanted to change or do anything about it. It took a long time before I started to invest in my health instead of just investing in my businesses and career growth.

By this time, I was around three years into working a very intense full-time agency job, running my wedding-planning business, co-running a wedding directory and online shop, and taking up photography. I recall chatting with a business mentor and her warning me that just because I could do all the things didn't mean I needed to "do all the things." I recall thinking, "Oh yeah? Watch me." Spoiler alert: I should have listened!

For many years, I constantly said, "I don't have time" for this or that. It wasn't until someone pointed out to me that *we prioritize what we value most* that I fully realized that I valued my income and job more than most things in my life. I valued work more than my health, my well-being, and my relationships.

I finally decided I was no longer okay with living that way and needed to change my habits to find myself outside of my job. I no longer wanted to wear my burnout like a badge of honour. It definitely wasn't going to be a quick fix, but I knew I needed to make changes.

When the COVID-19 pandemic hit, I luckily had the opportunity to work from home. With the uncertainty of the event industry, my day job was back to a manageable schedule while we recalibrated. Although I was fortunate to keep my job, I soon started to lose all my wedding planning and wedding photography clients for summer 2020. I was stressed AF and had a lot of extra time on my hands . . . cue the anxiety.

Only this time, instead of pouring myself back into work, I decided I was going to take the extra freedom I was given and focus on my health. For the first time in years, I finally had energy to be back in the kitchen, try new workouts, and slow down. I had always been in hyperspeed mode, feeling like I was behind. It was the first time I felt I was starting to find myself outside of work again.

My constant overbooked schedule had a poor impact on my eating habits, sleep, mind, and movement. I knew I needed some extra help to guide me on my wellness journey. I booked a virtual appointment with my naturopath and started to work through the challenges I was facing.

In addition to seeing my naturopath on a regular basis, I signed up for a virtual personal trainer who helped me maintain a routine with weekly check-ins. Between the two of these ladies, I felt completely supported in my wellness journey.

I started thinking about how I wanted to live post-lockdown. What did I truly value in life and what did I want to give my energy to? How could I have a healthy relationship with work?

I decided I wanted to focus on becoming the healthiest version of myself. I wanted to value my wellness before the money in my bank account or my busyness. This change didn't mean that success in my career was no longer important to me, it just meant that I wouldn't take on a new client or extra projects if I had to sacrifice my mental or physical health. The word "boundaries" finally became a part of my vocabulary. For a people-pleasing YES girl, putting boundaries in place took A LOT of practice.

I knew I could only have longevity in my new business if I focused on myself first.

From a point of burnout, I began to refill my cup. I finally felt creative again. I couldn't stop thinking about new business ideas and how I wanted to expand as an entrepreneur. I had been so busy that it wasn't until I slowed down that I realized I didn't want to be a part of the event and wedding industry anymore. I wasn't meant to work for someone else. I was destined to be my own boss.

Rest provided me with the clarity I so desperately needed. All this time I had been so afraid of "rest" that I had avoided it at all costs. From this point of clarity, Vanessa West + Co was born: a boutique brand agency that would break free from the hustle and grind culture and work from a place of ease and abundance.

A part of me had always wanted to dive further into branding photography and web design, as it was the side of my business I enjoyed the most. I also loved helping other businesses just starting out with these elements. From day one, I should have seen the signs that I was happier building my website and planning brand shoots compared to planning and coordinating weddings.

I realized that staying in the wedding and event industry would not allow me to live the wellness-first lifestyle I wanted. It is a high-stress job, no matter how organized and efficient you are. Although I am strong under pressure and would often be complimented that I was "cool as a cucumber," I no longer wanted to be in a job where I was required to internalize so much stress. I now truly believe that finding my love for event planning and entrepreneurship was meant to lead me to photography and web design.

As much as I was excited and ready to jump into launch mode ASAP (I am an Aries), I knew I could only have longevity in my new business if I focused on myself first.

I promised myself that I wasn't allowed to launch another business until I made my health my number one priority. With help from my naturopath and personal trainer, I finally made that happen!

Starting this business was different from my last. I was done with playing small and was ready to invest in myself and value my time and energy. I was sick of climbing the corporate ladder and trying to convince employers of my worth. I felt the drive and confidence that I was unstoppable.

Around the same time that I was having these realizations, I began to learn about positive affirmations and limiting beliefs. I took a virtual self-hypnosis program to shift toward a new, positive and empowering financial mindset. This program was an absolute game changer for me. It allowed me to discover myself and my money mindset on a deeper level, both personally and professionally.

I had no idea I was living with a "lack mindset." I worked through self-hypnosis and other programs to begin my shift into an "abundance mindset." Doing so allowed me to grow in my business by understanding my limiting beliefs. I started understanding my relationship with money and how others perceived money in business. It blew my mind! Understanding abundance and rewriting my beliefs allowed me to realize that my success and happiness is limitless. There is no cap. I can achieve anything.

Combining these learnings while working toward a wellness-first lifestyle had me feeling unstoppable. Finally understanding that I am worthy of all the happiness and success I desire, without burning myself out, brought on a whole new level of confidence. It was still scary as shit at times, but on those days I felt low or second-guessed myself, I took the time to rest and look inward.

With this newfound confidence, I started to invest in my business in a way I never had before. I invested in big-ticket courses and new equipment, and I signed a lease on my own creative space. I refused to let any fear of failure get in my way.

I had been dreaming of my own "space" for years, but I never fully understood what business that space would be for. I pictured a completely white space with tall ceilings and big windows in an old building downtown. Sure enough, I found myself scrolling through Instagram and saw an apartment listed with a local realtor. Instantly, my gut said, "This is it."

I reached out immediately to book a showing and got to view the space the next day. My whole body tingled with excitement. In the middle of a pandemic, I signed a lease and paid first and last with basically every dollar I had in my account. Despite my family once again telling me it was not the right time, I jumped in without looking back. I cried tears of joy while also being scared shitless. In a very similar way as the NYE party, I knew having this space was going to be the start of something great. I was ready to help other entrepreneurs build their brands.

At that point, I only had worked with three or four clients. Little did I know that I would be growing my business at an exponential rate and would soon make enough to cover a year's rent in nine weeks.

With this growth, I quickly had a full plate and started to slip back into my old work habits. I realized I needed more help before I went down the dark path of burnout again. I began to work with a habits coach to continue to help me understand myself on a deeper level and build healthy habits around work for the long run, not just short-term quick fixes.

A huge lesson for me has been to value your health and your time over anything else. No amount of money or approval is worth sacrificing your mental or physical well-being. Here are a few examples of changes I have made to work toward building healthier habits around work:

- Eat breakfast before opening emails or starting your workday. You can't pour from an empty cup.
- Keep your living/workspace tidy! Mess = stress.
- Move your body. Stretch and go for walks every day, even if it's just a quick loop around the block. That email can wait!
- Practice daily affirmations and gratitude.
- Create a relaxing bedtime routine without electronics.
- Write out your task list for the next day. This brain dump will allow you to have a better sleep.
- Be kind to yourself when life throws you off your routine. There is always a fresh start tomorrow!
- Ask for help when you need it.

When you put your health first, you will be able to show up as your best self in your business. You can work from a place of ease because you are not constantly burning yourself out.

A friendly reminder: Your self-worth is not based on your job title, accomplishments, or busy, overbooked schedule! Take care of yourself. There is no need to rush to check off each goal on your to-do list as if you are behind. In doing so, we forget to enjoy the process and journey of entrepreneurship.

Celebrate the little things. Enjoy the day-to-day. Take time to rest and enjoy life outside of work along the way!

For my husband: Thank you for always being my biggest cheerleader and reminding me that I'm a badass in those moments of self-doubt.

Vanessa West is a branding photographer and web designer based in Ontario. After launching her first side hustle in her early twenties, Vanessa fell in love with the process of starting a business and building a brand. After years of juggling multiple side businesses in addition to her full-time role at a Toronto marketing agency, Vanessa reached a point of complete burnout and knew she had to break away from the hustle culture she had fallen into. From a point of burnout, Vanessa began to refill her cup and put in the work to make her health number one while still kicking ass in her career. From this point of clarity, Vanessa West + Co was born — a boutique brand agency that would break free from the hustle and grind culture and work from a place of ease and abundance. After learning many lessons the hard way, it was important to Vanessa to include a wellness component in her business and share her experience with others to help them avoid continuous burnout and feelings of overwhelm. When Vanessa isn't working on all things web design + photography, you can find her practising self-care, spending time with her husband and fur babies, or hitting up her favourite local restaurants and shops!

"Finally understanding that I am worthy of all the happiness and success I desire, without burning myself out, brought on a whole new level of confidence. It was still scary as shit at times, but on those days that I felt low or second-guessed myself, I took the time to rest and look inward."

Vanessa West

Reflection Prompt

Create a list of things that you can do to help you recalibrate on those shitty days. What helps bring you back to centre?

How can you heal the insecurities rather than fill them?

Reflection Prompt

Have you been hiding your voice and your truth?

Why?

Chapter Eight

I Have a Voice

Ranika Singh

I was born in North York, Toronto. My parents were immigrants and transitioned to Canada during the mid-1970s. My parents were hard-working and always put their family first. My dad worked long hours; I remember how tired he was. My mom was always with us kids; it seemed everything she did was for us. I knew things weren't easy for them, but I always felt loved. They did the best they could, even with the challenges they encountered as immigrants. I spent most of my life in Scarborough, Toronto, living there from the age of two. I had a "normal" childhood, like most. I'm in the middle between two siblings. We were close and were always playing outside. We enjoyed the hot summer Toronto days. We were happy. I loved music—listening to strong female musicians has always been relaxing and a coping mechanism for me. I loved Whitney Houston, Cyndi Lauper, and Mariah Carey. One of my best memories was cheering for our city's baseball team during the playoffs, which had eventually led to a World Series win. I hold on to these memories and the times that I felt comfortable enough to express my joy. Although I loved my family and our days together, there was always some darkness overriding my childhood and young adult life.

I very rarely spoke outside my home environment, well, almost never. I remember being four years old and having another classmate get mad at me because I wasn't "active enough" in our playtime together in the sandbox. The thing is, I didn't know how to speak with her. All I can remember is feeling very anxious, not knowing how to precisely communicate with anyone. This anxiety, fear, hopelessness, and embarrassment were always there. I can still remember this day: it was the beginning of being called quiet and shy and hearing "she never talks!" and "she is just plain weird." No one in my family knew what to do, and I don't believe my teachers understood my actions either. Through my entire elementary school years, I didn't say a word. I barely participated in anything, and it just became normal for me to sit in silence. The few friends I had, the other "normal" kids in class, my teachers—everyone left me alone and didn't really push. I mean, by this age, I thought I was a pro at getting away with making excuses, not being expected to talk, and not initiating anything. But my grade 8 music teacher was different. She pushed me. She wanted us to practice singing the musical scale and then present it in front of the entire class. I didn't want to; I was so scared. I even had an excuse: I insisted that my hands were too cold to demonstrate the hand movements. She wouldn't give up and kept persisting, but in a way I hadn't felt before. It felt empowering, as she believed that I could really do it. So, I went ahead and sang, extremely embarrassed and then just happy it was done.

I remember that right before I started high school, I felt lonely. I didn't feel connected with any childhood friends or even myself. I knew I wanted to meet others, have friendships, and feel that I was a part of a group. I was tired of sitting at lunch tables and feeling that I had nothing to say during kids' random conversations. I remember always sitting on the edge, knowing how strange it seemed that I would "tag on" to groups but never really fit in. I remember this girl in my class one day. We were in some sort of elective class, maybe baking or sewing. She tried to communicate with me; I remember the way she looked at me. She was trying. It reminded me of the time in kindergarten, but this time, this girl didn't seem angry with me. She was kinder. I was older and could see the look in her eyes. She wanted to get to know me. But I still felt the struggle, the strong hesitance. I knew that I wanted to feel comfortable trying new things. I walked home that day, looking down the entire time and thinking of Mariah Carey singing "Hero" just for me.

I could feel that sense of comfort that I was learning to understand and develop during high school. I pushed it away for my entire childhood, but by high school, I realized that I needed to do more on my own. I just needed to always feel comfortable, then I would be okay.

So, I would speak up once, ask a question, hear a reply, and ask another question. Each step seemed so hard. Why was it so hard for me? At this point in my life, I knew I was different. The other kids didn't seem to feel what I felt. I still tried to see possibilities in my future, that I could truly be happy with myself one day. It is challenging to describe this moment in my life. I could see that I could engage and could speak. I was still so young, but I knew at that age that I had this inner strength that would always guide me. Even though I couldn't always show up as myself, I knew it was there inside. I just had to figure out a way to push and move past the anxiety, to just believe in my inner strength that I knew was there just below the surface. I knew my insecurities and inability to present myself or communicate could potentially continue to keep me away from what I loved to do most, which was meet new people and learn about them. People seemed so interesting. I craved more opportunities to connect. I believe these years tested and challenged me in a way I hadn't experienced before—I was now ready to learn to like myself.

I was now ready to learn to like myself.

By the time I graduated university and was ready to start my career, I was different. My early twenties were filled with experiences new to me. I went out more often with friends, took care of my appearance, and enjoyed laughing and having fun outside my home. I had been working as a waitress throughout university and although I disliked physical work such as waiting on tables and cleaning (I was lazy!), I loved having conversations with people. It felt so good to move freely from table to table, meet a newly engaged couple, or catch up with a group of friends who met up at our local café every Friday evening. I felt something new; I was being heard by them. It was a strange feeling, but it continued to spur something inside of me. It made me think that I had a purpose, that I could potentially be more myself. I felt better than I ever had at this point. I was ready for the next step. I was independent and ready to tackle the world!

With every new job opportunity, I became more comfortable in my words. I was still cautious about expressing myself, but I started learning about team dynamics and having colleagues. I learned about policies and deadlines and how to manage multiple tasks. I liked working within the government sector. I wanted to feel that my contributions could make an impact on many people. As I reflect, the best moments were when I could visit different communities throughout Ontario and Canada and learn about their specific needs. I was comfortable in these settings. When I was able to connect with someone who trusted in me, that was when I was most engaged and happy.

However, I struggled with making decisions for many years of my career. For example, I didn't feel comfortable speaking up when I disagreed with a colleague's opinion or experienced a challenge. Perhaps this feeling is similar for many in professional settings. For me, I knew I wasn't the same person I was growing up. But why couldn't I communicate when I was overwhelmed or didn't understand? For some reason, I believed that I couldn't make mistakes. For years, this fear held me back; I always felt like I could be doing more but didn't know how to or believe that I deserved it.

As I mentioned, I absolutely love strong women musicians. Maybe it's the confidence they have that inspires me or perhaps it's the words they are so comfortable expressing. My favourite singer is Alicia Keys. In my early twenties, a time when friends and relationships can significantly affect your life and the decisions you make, her music connected with me. I felt she was going through all the same life obstacles, challenges, and joys as I was. Was she writing and singing for me? Wishful thinking, but it made me happy. Her music helped me through breakups, finding love, loving myself, and finding the strength to believe I am enough. Although many of my friends and family joke about my "obsession," I knew I would meet her one day, and that day came a few months after I turned thirty. I had signed up for a contest and won—I was going to have a "meet and greet" with her backstage at her next concert in Toronto. I had no idea what I would say to her, but I couldn't wait. I was so nervous and knew that I wanted to tell her that I LOVED HER! But how can you say that in a way so you don't embarrass yourself and look crazy, especially with bodyguards so close to you both? But I was honest and genuine. I told her how much I wanted to be like her one day. She said to me, "You're fine the way you are!" I wasn't satisfied, so I said, "No, you just inspire me so much." She didn't say anything, she just hugged me. It was a hug that could last a lifetime. I always think back about what she said to me. I sure didn't believe at that time and that age that I was fine! Was she serious? How could I be fine when I felt unsatisfied? I hadn't been living the life that I WANTED. I recognized insecurity, failure, fear, and lack of confidence in my inner voice. Although I had what so many could say is a happy life (family, marriage, home, and job security), I never felt I was at my full potential. I craved more.

Life was changing fast; I was getting older, I was maturing, and I was starting a family with my husband. When my daughter was born, my work ethic improved. I immediately felt more inclined to work as hard as I could. I had not known about the feeling I'd have when we started having kids. I didn't read about it, and none of my friends or family really spoke about it. Nothing made sense. It was confusing raising small kids and being a new mom, just as it was confusing when Alicia Keys told me I was fine when I didn't believe I was. What I did know was that my greatest wish was to always understand my children—to have them speak to me, even when they couldn't talk about or understand how they were feeling.

Throughout the next few years, I changed roles again. It was to be the last role with my previous employer. At this point, I still felt the same professionally. I was still grateful but saw the same lack of opportunity and growth for myself. But I was now working in a more one-to-one advising role with a new set of clients. I quickly learned how challenging this role became. I started getting attached to clients' timelines, goals, and setbacks. The more involved I became in their plans, the more it affected and motivated me. I wanted to do my best to help, as I saw many barriers.

I didn't realize how much my life would change by working with international medical graduates. I saw something I recognized in myself in the pain and perseverance they shared with me. I almost felt that the more I learned about their personal stories, challenges, growth, and accomplishments, the more I became healed. I'll never forget the time I was asked to start delivering sessions to larger groups. I was terrified! I had been managing my fear of speaking up for all these years, never really showing up as myself, but now I would be speaking in front of larger groups? How could I possibly teach them when I felt teaching them was something I just couldn't do? I tried anyway. My first session was thoroughly prepared, down to every note about my slides. I remember having thirty-plus pages of notes, but during the session, I somehow misplaced or shuffled a few pages. I was so embarrassed, and I felt my face turn bright red. I allowed myself to feel disappointment, but I quickly bounced back. I knew I had to find confidence; people with real hopes and dreams needed me to show up. I knew the information

I was presenting, I just hadn't fully acquired the skill set to present it in a larger setting. But the more experience I got, the more I improved. I started to fall in love with these sessions. It was a private space where I could feel secure, learn, and make connections with people I wanted to help. When I was alone in those larger boardrooms, sharing time through information and encouragement, I felt truly happy.

In 2018 I broke my ankle during an accident and underwent emergency surgery. This incident changed my perspective on life in many ways. Fortunately, I had never been physically injured before; my pain had always been internal. No one could see it, and I felt protected in that sense. But after breaking my ankle, I didn't know how long it would take for the physical pain to subside. I felt fragile and helpless, especially while taking care of my kids. When I was in the wheelchair for six weeks, or the following few months when I couldn't keep up walking with a friend, I tried to act like I was okay, but I was hiding—hiding my true self and the challenges I was experiencing. Most people were very kind and wanted to help. I saw the look of fear in some eyes. Instead of absorbing the fear, I looked outward. When I was recovered, I started walking, losing some of the weight I gained after having kids. I never knew the power of trees and the energy they can bring into your life. I watched one season move to another, seeing the differences and appreciating nature in a way that I wished I had done earlier. It was during this time that I learned my childhood anxieties had a name:

selective mutism. It was so overwhelming to read about the complex anxiety disorder, but I was fascinated that I felt understood. I was also very sad. But all I could do was continue going, moving, and healing.

Everything felt like it was happening at once. Despite having found comfort in a name for what I had experienced in my childhood, I was scared I would lose my position at work. There had already been cuts, and more were expected. We were all worried. A week before I was laid off, I went through all my notebooks and shredded them all. I cleared out a lot of my desk, not knowing that I would be completely clearing out my items the following week. But something nudged me to do it. It helped me when I left; I was emotional and needed to feel this closure to fully move forward in my life.

The ability to communicate with another and inspire self-reflection or change is so powerful.

I thought a lot about Alicia Keys during the days and weeks of that summer while being unemployed. I thought about how she made me feel when I watched her play the piano, and how I felt understood when I heard her words. I thought about myself and how I felt being connected to another person, how it made me motivated and inspired to continuing helping people in some way. The ability to communicate with another and inspire self-reflection or change is so powerful. I started feeling like I could really do the same. I wanted to empower others. I was already doing it with the clients I had been mentoring for a few years, and I could continue. But wait. *There was no team anymore; I don't have an employer anymore*, I thought. I knew this lack of employment meant I had to work harder and fight harder than before. I could just go for it! I had to make that decision. But on my own? How could I do it?

During those initial months, I worked on my résumé and searched for jobs, still unsure about what to do. Then, a past client contacted me, letting me know how thankful they were for me and how they wished the best for my future. It was nice. Suddenly I went from one client to five to maybe fifteen at some point. I felt so motivated, especially when a few of them also updated me on their progress and asked for my opinion. It felt so natural. I almost felt like there was no decision to be made, as my life was unfolding before my own eyes. I knew what I was going to do: continue working with a group of people who had helped me toward healing in the past and those who would help me toward growth in the future.

I enjoyed my new flexibility with work and jumped on the opportunity to volunteer during my son's junior kindergarten class trip to the local outdoor learning centre. After lunch and before we headed out for the nature walk, his teacher initiated a discussion about the students' knowledge of birds and animals they may see. I was so excited to see my son happy in class. But as I watched my son sit at the back of the class, he looked sad. He hadn't put up his hand to answer any of the questions. I whispered to him, "Are you okay? Do you want to say something?" He nodded yes. I told him he could do it, he just had to try. "I believe in you," I said. We still laugh about this memory because he did try! During the walk following the discussion, his teacher asked a question, and my son threw his hand straight up so quickly. He needed a reminder about the question being asked, but he still answered. It felt good to recognize his fear and be there for him that day.

Just when I felt the most strength and perseverance as ever, what happened next? The entire world learned about the COVID-19 pandemic. It was the beginning of 2020, and I had no idea how challenging the following year and a half would be for me. I remember spending nearly all of February 2020 just thinking about failure and fearing what others would say or think about my decision to start my business. I remember sitting on the floor that winter, on my soft grey carpet, and finding strength in myself with the assistance of Alicia Keys and her latest album. I knew that I would be seeing her in mid-August at her concert. I was motivated and looking forward to new opportunities. And then the news and reality of the pandemic really set in.

Everything around me and everyone I knew was panicking and worried. I was at home, still unsure of my next steps, while being primarily responsible for my two school-aged kids who were learning virtually.

My husband didn't have as much flexibility as I had. I was in shock like everyone, just trying to process the sudden change and lockdown we were in. But we tried; I continued going for walks for a few months, which helped me deal with the anxiety of the pandemic and the sudden overwhelming feelings of hopelessness I was experiencing. I knew I could only keep going. I had to find a way to continue believing in myself, my goals, and what I wanted to obtain. My strategy was to understand what I needed to know about the pandemic but not absorb the constant news and dreadful feelings of uncertainty. Instead of absorbing the fear, I looked inward. It was so challenging trying to balance my schedule and understanding what I should be doing next when I didn't even know how my kids' schedule looked. We kind of learned together. It's like they were my mini co-workers during the first year. My daughter learned my clients' names, and both kids often made an appearance at my many meetings. At some point, my daughter thought mommy's job was to ask people which ice cream flavour they would choose to be and why. What a beautiful life that would be. I was starting to believe it was mine somehow.

During one of the times our province wasn't in lockdown, I took my daughter to her favourite mall. We were in the bookstore and looking around when my daughter started looking through the Barbie collection. She asked why she couldn't find a doll that looked like her. I didn't know what to say. I knew I spent my entire childhood experiencing this same thing, but I hadn't even thought of questioning it while growing up. I was angry at first but told her everything was okay. We would speak up; we would use our voice. That evening, we sent an email to the store's head office and told them how we felt. Additionally, we spoke with the manager in the store. Eventually, after the next lockdown was lifted, we saw a difference. There was more diversity in the Barbie collection, and my daughter not only saw more of herself, but she was proud that she helped make it happen.

During the pandemic, I had this determination in myself like I had never seen before. I don't exactly know how to explain how it felt. I understood that this was my moment; I knew that if I wanted to explore my business and gain the experience I needed to learn and grow more within this role, I had to do it then. I couldn't let my pandemic anxiety or worries affect me. Pushing myself has not always been easy, especially when I've spent most of my life disappointed by my actions or "lack of action." How would I prove to myself that I am capable and worthy of the life I want? My greatest lessons during the pandemic were having more acceptance of my past, recognizing my weaknesses, and moving toward growth.

My business officially started at the end of 2020. I took my previous personal and professional experiences and put them in a business that supports international medical graduates with various health care career options, including medical licensure in Canada. I have met some wonderful people, as I continued to connect with more peers, excelled in excellent client relationships, and developed my business. But in any business, there are times when we are challenged and are facing conflicts. I've had to quickly learn how to be a leader. I've had to prioritize and make decisions that I would have easily been happy to turn away from just a few years ago. I didn't realize all the different hats you have to wear or how you can take every decision you make so personally. I've been improving in these areas. I know that my life experiences have enabled me to develop these skills and have provided me with a strong foundation for ongoing growth. I love meeting clients from all over Canada and connecting with those who are still international and planning their transition to Canada. I keep thinking about my parents here. Imagine if they received more support when they transitioned during the 1970s? Imagine if these services existed? Would it have prevented the obstacles and challenges they had? I don't know. But it's something that keeps me motivated.

As much as I put effort into others, I recognize that the same amount of commitment should be expected for me. I've seen myself this past year, and I recognized how I could be kinder to myself and develop stronger boundaries. I remember just a few months ago when the Toronto Blue Jays started their season, and my husband encouraged me to watch the game because it's one of our favourite things to do together. I didn't watch though, as I was in a state of constant "go." I was feeling tired and needed a good vacation before I felt like I was allowed to start relaxing. I caught myself in the same situation that I advise my clients to avoid. I'm still learning how to live a more balanced lifestyle. Work hard but play harder. Well, I can say now that I finally know the Jays' starting lineup, and I'm excited for the rest of the season. I have to keep reminding myself that I deserve to be happy right now.

What's next? I'm not exactly sure, but I'm excited. I understand that I'm still figuring out my life and my future. But I'm okay with waiting; I'm okay with it being a process. My own personal journey has been healing and empowering. That voice that has been so hidden, hiding from everyone, including me, is here—right now. I can feel it in every word I've written here, in every new inquiry I reply to, and in every instance when I encourage my children that they, too, have their own voice. Finally, I've realized that I am enough, and I am just getting started.

I would like to express my sincerest gratitude to my family, friends, and peers for their ongoing support and guidance throughout my life. I feel truly blessed to experience such beautiful relationships with you. Thank you to my mother, who has always shown me the true meaning of perseverance, and to my father, who has shown me how true kindness is so beautiful. I would like to dedicate my chapter to anyone who has ever felt like they weren't good enough or felt like an underdog. Show up as yourself and, more importantly, love yourself first. If you don't love yourself first, no one else will.

Ranika Singh is the owner of IMG Career Counselling, where she coaches international medical graduates to achieve their goals through a strong combination of her love of counselling and her professional expertise. She demonstrates strong leadership, partners in a national campaign, and advocates for an equal chance to work in Canada. She is a daughter, sister, friend, wife, and proud mom to two beautiful, energetic children. There is nothing more important to her than being her true self and believing she is enough. She's been through a lot and no longer denies it. After experiencing nearly four decades of hiding her truth and suffering through a complex childhood anxiety disorder that has followed her throughout her life, she is healing and building on her strength to advocate for awareness of this rare disorder and the long-term effects it has if left untreated. Ranika loves everything from creating fun and empowering storyboards to painting her next abstract expressionist piece. She once created a storyboard poster that was featured twice during the live telecast of the Toronto Raptors Championship Parade. It was even held up and signed by Nick Nurse, the head coach, during the parade! And performer Drake gave Ranika's daughter, who was holding the poster, some big smiles that day! Empowering others is important to Ranika. Her greatest mentor, musician Alicia Keys, has strongly influenced her for more than twenty years. Ranika has even met her! Ranika volunteers her time supporting and mentoring high school girls facing multiple barriers. Together, they are building a diverse network of talented, vibrant women and girls to inspire and support one another. www.imgcareercounselling.com LinkedIn Ranika Singh

"I absolutely love strong women musicians. Maybe it's the confidence they have that inspires me; perhaps it's the words they are so comfortable expressing."

Ranika Singh

Reflection Prompt

What songs inspire you today?

What is it about these songs that inspires you?

If you tapped into this energy every day, how would it support you in making empowering decisions?

Integration Task:

Go belt out that song that just gives you all the feels!

Reflection Prompt

What are your major fears about starting a business?

List them all! Big or small!

Chapter Nine

Not Fearless, But Brave

Danielle St John

As a registered social service worker, I always dreamt of opening my own practice someday. After graduating from my social work program in 2014, I landed a great job, and my dreams of opening my own practice quickly took a back seat. I loved this job, I was making a steady income, I quickly moved up to senior level staff, I was happy, I was comfortable, and I thought I was going to be there forever. In 2017 the rug was quickly and abruptly pulled out from under me when my position no longer ceased to exist due to circumstances beyond my control. It was something I never saw coming, something that ended up being the greatest gift in disguise. I was lost at the time, and I didn't know what my next step was going to be. I had a mortgage to pay, children to support, and no job. After some time of sitting in my victimhood, I remembered that dream I always had, the dream of opening my own practice and running programs for women and youth. But wait, before

I could do that, I needed to take a few more courses and get a few more certifications, then I'd be ready to go. For the next two years I did just that—I took the courses, I became certified in multiple modalities, I hired a business coach, I mapped out my business, I had a plan, I got everything in place, and I was ready to go! In January 2019 I took the big leap and decided to start my own practice, and I registered Self-Empowerment Counselling & Coaching Services. Finally, I did it! Now what? It hit me: I'm here, this is what I've always wanted, I've spent so much money to get here (insert imposter syndrome), so who was I to be doing this job? Was I educated enough? Did I have what it took? Was I the right person for the job? The fear was real, and man, was it strong! I spent the next year in "business," developing programs, creating a website, and yes, taking more courses . . . talk about procrastination! In the coaching and self-development world, we are often told to be fearless, to think positively, and to trust the process. Don't get me wrong, this advice is all valid, but when you aren't trusting yourself, you don't feel "enough" or worthy of your dreams, thinking your way positive won't work. Your brain is like "What is this bullshit?!" Subconsciously, we are carrying limiting beliefs that are holding us back and keeping us stuck, and just simply thinking positively and slapping an affirmation on it just won't cut it. We have to do the deep work, so that's what I did. I hired a coach, not for business but for my own personal development. I looked at my shadows, I uncovered what was holding me back, and I took programs that would help me grow and expand so I could truly and authentically show up for myself in my business. At the beginning of 2020, I co-created a program for youth called Resources for Resilience. Youth signed up, the space was booked, we were ready to go, and bam! PANDEMIC. You have got to be kidding me. My initial reaction was defeat, and along with it came all the stories I would tell myself: *Maybe this isn't meant to be. Maybe I'm not meant to be running my own business.* I sat with it for a bit; I was angry, sad, and frustrated; I was ready to quit and then I remembered my worth, my value, and my strength. The year 2020 became one of pivot for me. I stood up, dusted myself off, straightened my crown, and stepped the fuck into my power. With everything so out of control, I had to ask myself, what was within my control? We quickly shifted the program online, which allowed us to reach a greater population. I started using social media as a platform to be seen, to connect, and to have conversations. My phone started ringing for client appointments, my income more than doubled, I was asked to run a master class and to be a speaker on a podcast, all during a global pandemic! And why? Because I started to believe in myself and stopped looking for external validation. I started listening to the whispers and the nudges so I didn't have to endure the screams. I learned to trust my intuition and started showing up every damn day. A coach once said to me, "Don't consume more than you create." That's what I was doing, and it gave me an excuse not to step up and take action. The fear of being seen was debilitating. *What if people don't like me? What if they don't sign up for my programs? What if they don't want to work with me?* The only energetic difference between excitement and fear is "what if it does" and "what if it doesn't." My two most recent programs, Not Fearless But BRAVE: How to Feel the Fear and Do It Anyways and Straighten Your Crown are my greatest projects yet. I'm so grateful to be able to share my story with other women who might feel frozen in fear from taking a step toward what they want. I can only hope to be an inspiration as I help guide women through their own journey of self-growth and transformation.

Both faith and fear require us to believe in something we cannot see, so if we are making it up anyway, why not make it magical and focus on what we want? I know I am, and I'm just getting started!

It was the fall of 2015, and I was working a job that I absolutely hated when I got the call about a counselling position I had applied for. I couldn't be happier. It was my dream job, I was set, it was a place I had always wanted to work, and finally, I was there. It was a dream come true.

I loved my job, my clients, and my co-workers. I had my own office, my own extension, and my own business cards. I was happy, I was comfortable, I gave my all to this agency and my clients—to everyone but myself.

After my first year, I started to notice that I was burning out, and I was questioning my abilities. I felt like something was missing, but I didn't know what. I have always been an empath and knew from a very young age that I was on this earth to help and support people, so why did I feel empty?

In 2017 I was given an opportunity to attend a pilgrimage in Angers, France, through my work. It was a trip that would completely change the trajectory of my life. It was the first time I had ever chosen to do something for me. I was hesitant to accept the offer and leave my family for three weeks, but something inside me said to go. I didn't know at the time that it was my intuition guiding me to something bigger. (I have since learned to listen to those nudges without questioning them.)

I arrived in Angers in April. During the pilgrimage, we were taken back to the place the agency I worked for had started, we learned about its roots and foundation, and we heard about the life and history of the woman who began it all.

Her name was Saint Mary Euphrasia, better known as SME. Long story short, SME was a four-foot-nothing powerhouse of a woman who had a vision to support other women and children and found a way to make it happen with all odds against her. Due to widespread poverty after the French Revolution, women and children were left to fend for themselves, as the men had to leave home to join the military and sadly, many never returned. Saint Mary Euphrasia recognized the need for more housing for refugees. She had a gift of attracting like-minded people who shared her passion for justice, but her journey was not easy; it was one of struggle, hardship, resilience, faith, hope, belief, and pivots. With support, SME founded the Sisters of the Good Shepherd.

... I knew I was meant to be doing so much more.

Saint Mary Euphrasia's urgent appeal for refugee housing was denied many times. You see, in the 1800s, it was forbidden for nuns to be seen in their habit in public. Due to the law, SME had no way to bring these women and children to safety without being visible. Therefore, with the support of the bishop, SME and the rest of the sisters dug a tunnel under the road to link the mother house to the Abbey of St. Nicholas. There, they welcomed young women and children in need, and the house of refuge was started.

Why am I sharing this story? Hearing it was a pivotal moment in my life, the moment when something shifted in me, and I knew I was meant to be doing so much more. Take religion out of the equation. This was a woman who had a dream, a passion, and a desire to help and support people in need. She was told no, she was met with obstacles, and she had to learn to pivot, change directions, and find a new way to make her dreams happen. She was resilient and determined. She inspired me to take action on everything I had been holding myself back from.

When I returned home from this trip, I knew I had to take the leap and follow my dream to start my own business, but fear was setting in like a heavy weight resting on my shoulders. How was I going to make it work? I was so comfortable where I was. I loved my job. Was I being selfish? I had a family and children. Would starting a business be too risky? I decided to settle. I stayed in my job and put my dream on the back burner once again. There were too many what ifs, and the pressure of having it all figured out was too real. I needed a plan, the blueprint with all the details so I knew it would be a bulletproof plan with no chance of failure (which is so unrealistic, but I'm a Virgo, and I LOVE details and plans!). I also love to control the outcome. If you can control the outcome, then you can predict the future and make sure everything goes as planned, right? WRONG!

The universe had a different plan for me and none of it was in my lists or sticky notes! If I wasn't willing to move on my own, the universe was going to make me move. Talk about being tested! As I stated earlier, my position suddenly ceased to exist due to circumstances beyond my control, something I never saw coming. I was devastated, and it hit my ego hard! Maybe I was right in questioning myself and my abilities.

The victimhood also hit me hard. All my self-doubts and insecurities were setting in. I went on employment insurance, and I applied for multiple jobs, most of which I didn't want and many of which I declined interview requests because I was questioning my worth and whether I were good enough. I finally ended up taking a job, I was paid well, the people were great, and I had a lot of flexibility, but there was such a huge part of me still missing. There was that voice that kept pushing me toward following that dream to start my own practice.

This is the part of my life when I entered the "never-ending learning" phase. I said to myself, "Okay, I now have flexibility, so if I take some courses, hire a business coach, and create that 'blueprint' with all the details that I love so much, then I'll be ready. When all the puzzle pieces are in place, I'll take the leap." And that's exactly what I did. In January 2019 I registered my business, and for the next two years, I took courses, I became certified in multiple different modalities and therapy tools, I spent tens of thousands of dollars on programs and business coaching, and news flash! It changed nothing! I had plans and goals and developed programs, but there was no action. Sure, I registered a business, but I wasn't showing up. I wasn't showing up because what I needed wasn't in the programs and the coaching—I had to heal something within me.

I was carrying so many limiting beliefs that had followed me my whole life and were now showing up for me in my business. I was questioning who I was and whether I was worthy and deserving to hold the souls of individuals in my hands. Who was I to support and guide people on their journey of self-development when I was still trying to navigate my way through my own? I was so afraid to show up and be seen. The fear was so strong, like heart-pounding, palm-sweating, nervous-jitters type fear.

I knew if I was going to make it work, I had to first heal the parts of myself that were holding me back. I spent some time looking inward and understanding all the parts of me. I wasn't broken; I didn't need to be fixed.

I wasn't broken; I didn't need to be fixed.

There were points in my life when I was told I was too much and not enough at the same time. I was told that those ideas, thoughts, and dreams I had were "crazy" and that I would never make it work. I carried the burden of everyone else's fears and took them on as my own; the doubt became heavy. What if those people were right? What if I don't have what it takes?

It took time, but I realized that everyone was going to have an opinion no matter what choices I made, and the reality was that their opinions didn't even have anything to do with me, they were just projecting their own fears, regrets, hesitations, reservations, and limiting beliefs. In reality, I was the only person standing in my own way. I had to ask myself whether I was going to be the type of person who let someone else tell me if I could or couldn't do something.

I had two choices: I could either let the voices of other people hold me back, or I could stand in my power and choose me.

I needed to do what was best for me. Those who know me know I have never made linear choices in my life, so why start then? I decided

I'd rather have an imperfect plan and take messy action than wait around for things to fall into place and be perfect.

The reality was that waiting for things to be perfect in order to make moves was just an excuse for me to stay in my comfort zone. I mean, who doesn't feel safe in their comfort zone, right? But that's not where the magic happens.

In January 2020 I co-created and launched my first program, a year after registering my business. The venue was booked, participants were signed up, I was ready, I was excited, and I felt confident and scared all at the same time, but I was finally doing it and then the global pandemic hit. I felt so defeated. All this work, self-development, and business creation, then another boulder was dropped in front of me. What was happening? Hadn't I been tested enough?

I was upset, mad, and frustrated, and I honestly felt like giving up. Maybe it was a sign; maybe my business just wasn't meant to be. I sat with it for a bit, contemplating giving it all up.

I was reading people asking all over social media, "How are you going to answer the call? How will you use all this 'free' time you've been given to be productive?" WHHHHAAATTTT?!?! The call? How was this a call? This pandemic was completely fucking up all my plans!

Little did I know that I was answering the call. Everything this universe was giving me was something I was strong enough to handle, which didn't mean I had quit, it meant I needed to pivot and be flexible. As I previously mentioned, I like plans, notes, blueprints, and all the details! I pulled up my socks, straightened my crown, and started brainstorming how to make my business work in the middle of a global pandemic and province-wide lockdown. I quickly shifted my program online, created digital workbooks, became familiar with social media, and learned how to advertise and show up in ways that felt like foreign territory.

During the pandemic, I more than doubled my income, increased my clientele, and created two additional programs: Not Fearless, But Brave and Straighten Your Crown, all while also working full time with the school board and being a mom.

Now, I want to be clear: this journey has not been easy. I have run multiple programs throughout this time that no one signed up for. I have run masterclasses that had two people in them. I have done a Facebook Live that no one has watched, but here's the thing: I showed up anyway. I showed up and did the Live with no one watching, I created the program with no attendees, I did the Facebook and Instagram posts with no likes or comments.

So, you ask, what worked? Consistency! That's it, friends. Consistency—showing up every damn day, no matter what! Not letting those moments when no one signs up for your programs or shows up for your Lives take you out. It's the consistency that creates success. How can you possibly fail if you never quit? Become a "no matter what" person and always show up!

I realized that entrepreneurship is not linear, and those who tell you so are lying! Entrepreneurship is full of ups and downs, highs and lows, wins and hurdles, things that work and things that don't, pivots and lessons. Sometimes, you need to head back to the drawing board and completely shift. Do it!

Find your community. This is key! Find the people who expand you. Find the people that are being, doing, and having what you want and use them as evidence that you can be, do, and have it too.

I spent a lot of time during this process trying to perfect someone else's strategy, thinking that I would be successful in my business if I did it the way that worked for them. WRONG! No one was buying it, and clients called bullshit fast. When I finally showed up as my true authentic self and did it my way, that's when my phone started ringing. People want to know who you are, all the parts of you: the good, the bad, and the ugly. People want to know that you are a human being in a human body having human experiences to which they can relate. People don't want to see the glorified version of you, they want to see the real you.

Take the opinions of others for exactly what they are: opinions. Words and situations only become a big deal when we attach meaning to them. Take every situation as a lesson to grow and expand. Someone will always have a strategy that works for them: the "10-step program" to grow your business. Take what you need, leave the rest, and show up as you. The right people will always find you.

That thing you are afraid of is the thing you need to be doing. That thing you are avoiding is what your soul craves. Everything you have is already in you. If you are waiting to be ready, confident, have more time, money, or energy, you will be waiting a lifetime. Confidence comes from successfully completing a calculated risk. Confidence comes from consistency and showing up, even when you are scared and don't feel like it. You go first!

Pay attention to the little things: the signs, the whispers, the nudges—that feeling in your gut that tells you to do it before your ego sets in.

- Start before you feel ready because you will never feel ready.
- Launch the business without all the answers.
- Write the book. You don't need anyone to approve your story.
- Record the podcast. You don't need top-of-the-line equipment or movie set lighting.
- Show up for the Facebook Lives, even if no one is watching.
- Say yes to opportunities before you know what you're doing.
- Clap for yourself when no one else is.
- Celebrate the small stuff.

You can't fail if you never quit, and you can't succeed if you never start.

During my trip to Angers, I met a woman from New York. During one of our lunches, we started talking about some of our similar life experiences, and she leaned down, pulled a book from her bag and

All I had to do was dare greatly and be brave enough to walk the darkness to discover my light.

handed it to me. She held the book in her hand and told me she had brought it with her with the intention of passing it on to someone else. She handed me the book and said, "I think you need this more than I do." It was *Daring Greatly* by Brené Brown. I had never heard of Brené Brown before, but I kindly accepted the book, thanked her, and put it in my bag. I didn't open that book for six months. It wasn't until after I was no longer at my dream job that I remembered it. I grabbed it from my bookshelf, opened it, and the first quote I saw was: "Only when we're brave enough to explore the darkness will we discover the infinite power of our light."

You see, I didn't realize it at the time, but all these things weren't happening to me, they were happening for me. Pieces were falling apart so that the right pieces could fall into place. All I had to do was dare greatly and be brave enough to walk the darkness to discover my light.

Everything in my life has been placed there on purpose, almost like a puzzle being put together. All the people, the experiences, the good, the bad—every person I have ever crossed paths with—were all there for a purpose. It all had meaning.

What I've learned is that the storms, the hardships, the failures, the times we hear no, the times we fall—these are what make us stronger and more resilient.

I have continued to follow Brené Brown's work since I read her quote that day. She has been a guiding inspiration in my own work. I will leave you with the following from her:

"There will be times when standing alone feels too hard, too scary, and we'll doubt our ability to make our way through the uncertainty. Someone, somewhere will say, 'Don't do it. You don't have what it takes to survive the wilderness.' This is when you reach deep into your wild heart and remind yourself, I am the wilderness."

To my boys, Austin and Nick. There is no me without the two of you. You have taught me resilience and have brought me the immense strength I've needed to keep going. Thank you for being you. Thank you for teaching me more about myself every day. I am forever grateful you chose me to be your mom. I love you more than words.

To my family, each and every one of you, thank you for your unwavering support and unconditional love. Thank you for always standing in my corner, even when I didn't make it easy.

Danielle St John is a registered social worker, a self-empowerment coach, a spiritual entrepreneur, and a mom of two amazing boys. Danielle is trained in many modalities, including neuro linguistic programming, trauma, time line therapy, reiki, and QCP. Danielle always knew she was called to the helping profession, and in 2009, she decided to embark on her educational journey in social service. Quickly after graduation, she jumped straight into her career, landing what she thought was her dream job as a counsellor at a social service agency that supported young mothers. Although this seemed like the perfect job, something felt off. In April 2017 Danielle was given the opportunity to attend a pilgrimage in France, an experience she didn't realize at the time would change her life. It was a work trip; however, it turned out to be much more than that. "Something changed in me when I was in France; I don't know what, but I felt it. I felt a pull to do something more, something bigger, and I knew it had to start with healing myself first." Upon returning from France, Danielle decided to start living her life with intent and unapologetically going after all her dreams and desires. Today, Danielle is the proud owner and operator of Self-Empowerment Counselling & Coaching Services, where she works with individuals, helping to guide and support them on their journey through personal growth and transformation.

www.daniellestjohn.com

FB danielle.stjohn.79

"What I've learned is that the storms, the hardships, the failures, the times we hear no, the times we fall — these are what make us stronger and more resilient."

Danielle St John

Reflection Prompt

Head back to your fears and ask yourself:

Is this real?

What is the worst that's going to happen?

Can I handle that when (or if . . . but most likely when) it does happen?

How would it make me stronger and more resilient in the long run?

Reflection Prompt

What are the stories around money that you are carrying?

Chapter Ten

The Legacy

Sarah Vaill-Ciano

Sometimes, it's the legacy that we didn't even know existed before us that is the driving force behind the nudge in the direction of the unknown.

A newspaper article landed in my lap recently. This article "New book will focus on booming Main St." was in a local Newmarket publication on October 21, 1986, and in it, my father is described as "a printer, turned printing foreman and to a moderately successful publisher of local Authors," which was something I didn't know until this article made it into my hands. I knew that my father had always been involved with printing and graphic design, but I never understood at what capacity. I had been told a million times about the story when my mom bought a printing press while she was pregnant with me. What I didn't know is that in the same article, it was cited that "Karen—watching her own husband's success in the arts and publishing circles—has decided to take matters into her own hands at the age of 23. She is going to be a publisher herself." This article had a picture of my mom—short hair, buttoned-down shirt, very pregnant with me. I could see all the promise that lay behind her best-laid plan to create a life that would be far beyond anything she could even dream for her children. I can see that despite the difficulties I know my parents faced, they were trying to create a legacy that would be far outreaching to anything that they had grown accustomed to, and although I never got to see either of my parents in that capacity, I know deep down inside that my drive to change things for my children has always been a continuation of the foundation that they laid before me, even if they had to start over, again and again.

Growing up in poverty gave me a different appreciation for many things. I grew up dreaming of what could be; I strove to get out of where I was. I had big plans to take over the world, be rich and famous, drive a fancy car, and change the world. I dreamt BIG because I already knew what living small felt like. Although through most of my childhood my parents battled with addiction, money issues, and trying to raise four children, they were embracing their artistic roots, creating this wonderfully magical focus on the arts. My dad worked in printing when my sister and I were younger. He would create letterhead for our "businesses" that we ran out of his basement apartment. Our favourite, Ghost Club. My sister was the president, and I was the vice president. My sister would write scary stories about how someone had spotted a ghost in the area, then we would head into the forest (backyard) to locate it and bring it home to dispose of (think Ghostbusters, ha ha). My mom encouraged freedom of expression by bringing home four-foot by thirty-foot rolls of paper and covered all the walls to allow us to paint or draw as the mood hit. Both of my parents are artists and lovers of the written word. My life was surrounded with books, pictures, and tables littered with journals. We lived the starving artist life, quite literally. My mom went back to school when I was about seven when she was accepted in the Ontario College of Art and Design for Media Arts. My dad was a printer/typesetter and graphic designer when that was still a highly sought-out career, even though his aspiration to be his own business owner never really died. Picture a college-student budget and raising three kids on it. I saw persistence in the face of adversity, but I always saw that no matter how hard you worked, there was never getting ahead. I learned that you can work yourself into the ground, but you will never have what you need.

I started to create a plan. I knew that I didn't want the struggle the way I saw my parents do so continually throughout my whole life, so I started to avoid it in the only way I knew how: I worked. I got a job. I went to school all day, and I worked in the next town over every night. I would finish school and hop on a bus, then walk about fifteen minutes to get to work. I'd then do it all over again on the way home, usually doing homework on the bus after work. When I started making my own money, the downside for me was that I led a life with a scarcity mindset without even realizing it. Having my own money allowed me to have the things I didn't get in my everyday life. I could buy myself clothes, I could get a cellphone, I could buy my own food. So, I worked more, but there was never enough—food, money, time, love, stuff. I had this idea imprinted in my mind that if I didn't work hard, I was not worth anything, and I was only as good as my last accomplishment. Go to school, get good grades, make money, and continue to be a good member of society. It's like running a race backward; you are constantly moving in the right direction, but you just can't see the stuff you are tripping on until you have already fallen, and detours are inevitable. I was scrappy, hard-working, and dedicated because I needed it more than "they" did. I had a can-do attitude because I had lived through what felt like impossible times and had a small mouth to feed by nineteen.

Once I got into the workforce after college, I learned quickly that you just need to keep your head down, plow through, don't complain, and just work harder than the next guy. I was a typical "employee." I gave everything I had to jobs that wouldn't have tossed water on me if I were on fire because I needed the money to survive. Living in a constant state of stress wreaked havoc on my nervous system while I was going through my divorce, and I was working every spare moment to somehow keep my head above water. I had created this persona that I wanted people to see. I never wanted people to look at me or my children and see the struggle. I handcrafted this self-image that I would present to the world. I would put on a smiling face, and I would get to work, only harder now because to struggle like I did growing up was not an option. I was living in a constant state of fear of failure, and it was treacherous to my health and well-being. I had realized that I could do a lot, but I couldn't do everything, especially if I did it all out of fear. I started to step away from the mindset of never having enough to learn to recognize the abundance that filled my life, and in those small moments, everything changed. I started to look at my life and practice gratitude. Something so easy that after I worked all day, got the kids home, made dinner, did our bedtime routine, and cleaned the house, when I finally sat down at midnight after being up since 5:00, I would count my blessings. I started to take the small things in when I was struggling with exhaustion and fear. I would get up ten minutes before the kids, make my coffee, and sit on the steps out in front of my house to watch the sun rise and tell myself how grateful I was to provide the living that I do for my children. I started reworking the scripts that my parents were never able to, understanding that growing up, especially in the time they did, society always taught that success = money = power, and without it, you hold no worth in this world. Generations before us never questioned this logic, they just instilled and ingrained a go-go-go mentality in our minds. I struggle with this mentality to this day. I am a recovering perfectionist, and within my life and business now, I have had to stop and take stock of the moments when I know my money script leads the way instead of being in alignment with myself. I started to heal the money wounds that growing up in poverty created, and I began to regain the parts of my money story that I had told myself for years and years. If you find that you feel like no matter what you do, it's never quite good enough or you give and give but find it hard to receive or even perhaps feel, you're on a constant treadmill of working or striving to improve yourself without stopping to smell the roses, then you, too, may need to examine your relationship with money. Practice self-compassion by acknowledging that you are always doing your best. And in any given situation, your best is all you can give. I let go of the expectations of myself, and I try to remember that I took on a lot of my beliefs when I was really young, and at that time, I didn't have a way of deciding whether the things I was choosing to believe were going to be helpful to me in the long term or understanding that my subconscious beliefs drive most of my behaviour. So, judging myself for carrying limiting or faulty beliefs is like blaming the patient for being unwell. It doesn't help. What does help is to focus on healing my deep inner wounds and limiting beliefs instead.

Practice self-compassion by acknowledging that you are always doing your best.

I thought on and on about

what wisdom-filled greatness I was going to write in this chapter. I wanted to impart all the lessons of the failures and triumphs that I went through and came out of on the other side, not necessarily on top, but definitely a better version. I stifled the rubble of the shoulda, coulda, wouldas and decided that the part of my entrepreneurial journey that has brought the most joy, love, and excitement was the legacy I was going to leave—the legacy that my parents tried to give me.

I am Sarah. I am a divorced and remarried, animal-loving, full-time office manager. I am a reiki master practitioner with her own practice, an owner and operator of my own clothing line, an active online membership mentor, as well as a published author. I have also had the honour of mentoring women who are going through dramatic life changes that allowed them to step into their inner confidence to make enlightened and empowered decisions about their lives.

Additionally, I am a mom, which is by far my favourite full-time position that I hold. I have been the successful CEO of Isabelle & Ethan Ltd. since 2006, seeing year over year growth and expansion within this company. Human Resources (me) tells me that we get very few staff (children and husband) complaints and overall morale is at an all-time high as we come into our fifteenth year. In our fourteenth year, we started to re-invest within our company to create a legacy that I hope will continue for generations.

My children have watched me create, run, and transition businesses handfuls of times in their short lives. For example, when I was freshly divorced, I went back to school to become a makeup artist so that I would be able to supplement my income on the weekends that they were at their dad's so that they wouldn't feel the sting of our family dividing. That idea spurred the knowledge I needed to create multiple businesses from that point on. My children were bound to catch the bug, as they are surrounded by movers, makers, and shakers in their everyday lives. It just so happens that it was my daughter, Isabelle, that it took hold of.

Isabelle is a very dedicated equestrian. She has her heart horse named Ranger, who she loves beyond words. We wanted her to get the most of this experience by learning to love, care for, and do the work that comes with riding and owning a horse. I was at every step trying to show my daughter the value of her time, energy, and money, and she became responsible for some part of Ranger's care. She used to pay for her one lesson a week by working at the barn or with saved money from birthdays and Christmas, but as she progressed as an athlete, she wanted to do more lessons, which then spurred the "get a job" conversation from each parent she approached.

So, that is precisely what she did, and Little Bay & Co was launched three days before her fourteenth birthday. It is named after her Little Bay horse, Ranger. It was like I was back at the beginning all over again. Isabelle took her love for her horse and developed an equestrian-centred clothing line for all the "horse girls" like her. We chatted about how the business would look. She listed out the type of clothing she wanted, what kind of printing would be used, and she got to work on designs. This is where the fun began—the trial and error and frustration that I got to watch from a different vantage point this time, all while being all too aware of the thoughts and feelings she was having. She learned the designs that wouldn't pull or press properly, so she headed back to the drawing board. I would usually let her find out the hard way at least once to encourage her to look at the problem differently. Once she developed something she absolutely loved, it was time to get it out there to see if other people did as well. We made enough for her best friend, her mom, and Isabelle and me, and we headed to the barn for a photoshoot! I got my first look at the gift I was giving my daughter through mentoring her through the process. I got to see how impactful my wisdom was from the struggle of doing something a hundred different ways before finally finding out the way it worked best. I got to see the joy and excitement each time someone expressed an interest in the items that she worked so hard to make, and I got to show her how to step back, rein in the feeling of having to "hustle" to keep making all the money, and lean into when she was tired or overwhelmed so that she could make the call to defer orders or put things on hold. It was important that she learned to create the understanding around how she was feeling about the work she was doing.

It all became very real when we posted these pictures on an Ontario equestrian site to gather interest about her product and she got more than a hundred orders in twenty-four hours. I don't think either of us felt that this product would take off out of the gate quite like it did. First, the excitement set in, followed quickly by absolute terror! "How am I going to do that much?" she said, looking at me with her big, blue, terror-filled eyes. Since we thought she would have a handful of orders, we decided to have a board meeting about how she would do this work efficiently. We called in the crew to help our girl with her very first sellout! She organized her orders, she placed her first order through the same company I use for my blank clothing. She determined how much vinyl she would need, and we got to have the conversation about gross and profit income. She watched her bank account fill up and then slowly deplete as she purchased her materials. Her aunt came to help pull vinyl, I showed and assisted her with heat-press, and she designed her thank you cards to include in all her packages. We had boxes and boxes of orders that left the house on a daily basis. Isabelle went to school all day and then got to work in our shop, finishing her orders afterward. She got to see a completely different side of one of the businesses I run, and she excelled. She is naturally in tune with the thoughtful aspects of being a business owner. She just does the stuff that makes the difference to the unknown person at the other end. Handwritten notes and the perfectly tied bows, for example. Her crowning moment in business was when she was away at a show jumping competition and saw her sweater on a fellow equestrian and was told it was her favourite sweater. I am not going to lie, the pride was REAL here. I could feel my smile go from ear to ear while I watched my daughter interact with someone who had only been a name over the internet moments before. I could feel tears in the corner of my eyes as she turned back to me and I saw the shock on her face like it was the first time she realized that her product was floating out in the big, wide world for all to see.

I've learned how to find a dream and do it despite everything.

There are a couple things Isabelle's story makes me think of, especially when I think back on my parents trying to make it all work.

Your hard work does, in fact, help those coming up around you. Your pearls of wisdom, your words of encouragement, and your showing up in whatever capacity you can all gives someone the courage to just keep going. I have been blessed by the people in my life that I get to call mentors. I have seen this "hard work" come in so many different forms. I've seen the grind at a "job" to provide for a family and the "doing it all"—school, work, kids. I've learned how to find a dream and do it despite everything. I've evolved my understanding around work and learned how to take a step back and to lean into the flow of learning to understand my limiting beliefs and how they steer the direction of my choices and how that made me feel.

I've learned that failure is just the stepping stone for us to keep going or for our children to have a leg up. By doing, trying, and achieving, or for things not going as planned, my parents were eliminating a hurdle that may have stopped me or someone else because we were shown what was possible. Every step that you take toward a new path in life, you are sweeping clear the notion that it isn't possible because they have seen you do it. Understanding that even if you are failing, your worth is never tied to the money in your pocket or the material objects you own. Your worth is based solely on how you feel about the person that you look at in the mirror each morning and the gifts and service you are sharing with this world.

Every time I started a business that created joy and a sense of well-being, I was showing my future generations where the keys to their own fulfillment hung. Doing so as young as you can is a gift that is ever expanding and abundant. Show them that you don't have to kill yourself for someone else to make a living and teach them to know their worth as a person so that they can command the respect they deserve for the service or work they provide. Have them realize and embody that there are infinite amounts of money to be made and teach them what their money scripts are so that they aren't trapped in the generation traps that came before them. Own the idea that waking up loving what you do isn't a pipe dream.

I believe that understanding the legacy you are leaving isn't reserved for just your biological descendants but for all generations you have encountered. The ripple effect that you show your nieces, nephews, etc., creates that wave that ignites the passion for them. I hope that the impact I leave in the lives of the women I work with will far extend past their lives into the lives of everyone they meet.

As I sit here with this news article in my lap, I am reminded that what I will be leaving will be far more than the money my businesses may provide my children. I see it as the persistence that was handed down from two generations before them. That in the face of adversity, anything is possible, and it is their birthright to take hold of. I have taken the next step for them. My parents laid the foundation, and I built the steps. I removed some of the obstacles so that my children can see that regardless of what profession they decide to pursue, they have the power to choose how that looks for them. I am excited for them to be able to make decisions based on how a situation makes them feel—right, true, good—instead of making them from a place of fear of fulfilling basic necessities like food, water, shelter, which is something that I truly believe my parents were trying to do for our family but too many obstacles got in their way. I am here to show my future generations that it didn't stop me, and I am just getting started.

To my parents, who continue to show us the next steps to living our dreams; and to my children, who lean into the lessons to create the life that dreams are made of.

Sarah Vaill-Ciano is a charismatic wife, mother of two, and rad pet mom whose contagious energy is a total force to be reckoned with! While taking a path well-travelled by many, from uncertain childhood to young motherhood to soul-crushing divorce, she found herself at a crossroads: "Let my experiences define me or let them align me." She made the decision to let it fuel her intuitive, compassionate, and authentic way of life. For years, Sarah has served as a helpful role model to those seeking inspiration, help, or advice. In 2018 she finally decided to own that role and be intentional about it. Sarah is a Holy Fire III Master Reiki Practitioner, plant mom, and serial entrepreneur. With her determination, quick wit, and passionate soul, she has let very little stand in her way of bringing to life her aligned-over-hustle way of living. Hand in hand with her family and her incredible sisterhood, she has launched her business as her outlet for personal growth and as a safe space for all to join, connect, heal, and align!

"I am here to show my future generations that it didn't stop me, and I am just getting started."

Sarah Vaill-Ciano

Reflection Prompt

What is your legacy?

FINAL WORDS

Hey, Legacy,

Thank you for showing up to this book and honouring the stories within these pages.

Thank YOU for giving yourself permission to reflect!

Take a moment to feel into the inspiration, the encouragement, and perhaps even the discomfort that you have taken from these words. It is our hope that this book stirred something inside you, that you felt pieces of yourself within these stories and that you will take this opportunity to explore what your soul is calling you toward today.

We hope that these stories landed with a sense of excitement and inspired confidence for you to take steps toward achieving your dreams!

Any desire that has been placed on your heart is there for a reason. Trust it!

Don't let this world exist without you shining brightly in your unique magic!

A message to the BOSSES that fill these pages . . .

Thank you for expressing your truth and inviting us into your business.

We are so grateful that you entrusted us with holding a safe space for your stories and are so incredibly proud of each of you for owning your power and reflecting it into the world in the ways that you do!

Love always,

Sarah and Lindsay ♥

Endnotes

Shaheeza Haji

Manson, Mark. *The Subtle Art of Not Giving a F*ck: A Counterintuitive Approach to Living a Good Life.* HarperCollins, 2016.

Kelly Jane Thorne

Vanwynsberghe, Marsha, et al. *Owning Your Choices: Stories of Courage From 8 Inspirational Women Around the World.* Prominence Publishing, 2020.

Danielle St John

Brown, Brené. *Daring Greatly: How the Courage to Be Vulnerable Transforms the Way We Love, Parent & Lead.* Gotham, 2012.

GCW PUBLISHING HOUSE

We aren't your average publisher! GCW Publishing House and Media Group™ is a Canadian woman-owned and operated publishing house that ignites courage and confidence in women worldwide and helps them write high-impact, non-fiction books that make waves, move mountains, blaze trails, and change lives! We combine the art of storytelling, connection, camaraderie, support, marketing, and public relations into the book-writing experience to provide our authors with the entire publishing process and beyond!

For more information on publishing, blogging, and podcasting opportunities, please visit: gcwpublishing.com

ALSO AVAILABLE NOW

THE SHE SERIES

The Great Canadian Woman is every woman. She is overcoming trauma. She is coming to terms with her intuition. She is changing careers and finding a new path. She is grieving while raising her children. She is overcoming racial injustices. She is removing mental health stigmas. She is finding her joy. She is raw and real. She is a light in the darkness. She stumbles and falls, but she rises by sharing her story and speaking her truth. Sometimes we need to break so we can rebuild. In the chapters of this book, these great Canadian women show you how to do just that through their intense vulnerability, massive strength, immense courage, and endless perseverance.

AVAILABLE NOW

SHE GRIEVES | SHE IS ENOUGH

SHE GRIEVES—A special edition of real-life stories written by women who have learned to navigate the tsunami of grief and rise above the storm. A collection that will inspire and give permission to find purpose and joy to those living with grief.

SHE IS ENOUGH—A collection of real-life stories from women who have realized their worth—stories that will encourage all women to trust their intuition and live their life on purpose.

COMING SOON SPRING 2022

NEXT IN THE SHE SERIES

SHE IS FULL OF FIRE—A collection of real-life stories of women who go against the grain, make the hard and unpopular decisions, and live boldly in their personal freedom.

SHE IS WORTHY—A collection of real-life stories of women who have overcome hurdles that once bruised their self-esteem, so they could lead their lives with courage and confidence.

SHE LIVES HER TRUTH—A collection of stories and lessons from resilient women on their journey toward trusting their inner knowing and living with intention.

ALSO BY GCW PUBLISHING HOUSE

THE GREAT CANADIAN WOMAN—
SHE IS STRONG AND FREE SERIES

An inspiring three-volume series of real-life stories from Canadian women who have overcome life adversities, found a way through seemingly impossible circumstances, and rose above their pain and tribulations. Their courageous stories will instill a sense of hope and empowerment in others so that they, too, can overcome their personal hardships and know they are not alone. These stories grant us all the permission to live fully, love deeply, and fight like hell in the name of happiness.